The Wildlife Gardener's Guide

By Janet Marinelli

Elizabeth Peters
DIRECTOR OF
PUBLICATIONS

Sigrun Wolff Saphire
SENIOR EDITOR

Gerry Moore
SCIENCE EDITOR

Joni Blackburn
COPY EDITOR

Elizabeth Ennis
ART DIRECTOR

Noreen Bradley
VICE-PRESIDENT,
MARKETING

Scot Medbury
PRESIDENT

Elizabeth Scholtz
DIRECTOR
EMERITUS

Handbook #189

Copyright © 2008 by Brooklyn Botanic Garden, Inc.

All-Region Guides, formerly *21st-Century Gardening Series*, are published three times a year at 1000 Washington Ave., Brooklyn, NY 11225.

Subscription included in Brooklyn Botanic Garden subscriber membership dues ($35 per year; $45 outside the United States).

ISBN 13: 978-1-889538-37-2
ISBN 10: 1-889538-37-X

Printed by OGP in China. Printed on recycled paper.

**Cover: Bumblebee on *Rudbeckia* 'Prairie Sun', a coneflower cultivar.
Above: Cecropia Moth on fern foliage.**

The Wildlife Gardener's Guide

How to Welcome Wildlife to Your Yard

It isn't really spring in my yard until the Palm Warblers arrive. These pint-sized song-birds with streaked breasts and rufous caps are among the first migrants to arrive at my Shelter Island, New York, garden. Come April, they feed on tiny emerging insects they find in the thicket of shrubs and wild cherry and sassafras saplings behind my house. In a few days, they're gone, replaced by Yellow-rumped Warblers, Black-and-white Warblers, and various vireos, flycatchers, and thrushes. As the season progresses, a variety of butterflies, Ruby-throated Hummingbirds, and myriad other creatures are drawn to the flowers, fruits, and other goodies in my garden. Without them, my yard would seem lonely and incomplete.

I've read a lot of wildlife gardening books over the years, and they are all big on gen-eralities—reduce the size of your lawn, plant native wildflowers, stop using pesticides, and so on—but distressingly short on useful specifics. That's why I wrote this book. It's divided into ten chapters, each one with step-by-step instructions for a garden proj-ect that will bring birds, butterflies, and other captivating creatures to your yard.

The ten projects described in these pages can be used to make an existing garden more attractive to wildlife, or to create a new planting from scratch. They will trans-form your property into a refuge that provides wildlife with all their daily needs: food, water, and safe places to hide, rest, and nest. You'll learn how to make your flower border a magnet for lovely swallowtails and hummingbirds. You'll discover how to create a "stopover garden" where weary warblers and other migrating song-

North American coneflowers attract butterflies like this Painted Lady. Regionally native plants are best for wildlife because they have coevolved and formed close relationships over time.

birds can rest and refuel. Providing water for wildlife can be as simple as putting an old-fashioned birdbath in your garden—you'll find information on this and other water features that are easy to install and easy on your budget. You'll also find advice on the best feeders, birdseeds, and birdhouses, as well as garden plans to follow. Each gardening project includes lists of plants with proven wildlife appeal in your region, organized by region for easy reference.

These and many other tips will enable you to create a garden that delights not only you but also beautiful and fascinating wildlife—no small accomplishment at a time when the plants and animals with which we share the land are facing increasing pressure from human activities. Today, quality wildlife habitat continues to dwindle at a rapid rate. Urban and suburban sprawl destroys natural areas; invasive plants from our gardens run rampant in the remaining natural habitats and replace the native plants upon which wildlife depend; and the overuse of chemical pesticides and fertilizers poisons their food sources and can kill butterflies and other beneficial insects.

The most important thing we can do for wildlife is to make sure that their natural habitats are protected and restored. But we can also ease the plight of beleaguered wildlife right in our own backyards. This guide shows how.

How to Make the Most of This Book

Two important concepts are the foundation for this book. The first is that plants and animals need each other to survive. Animals need the nectar, pollen, fruits, and other foods that plants provide. Most plants need animals for cross-pollination to reproduce successfully. The second major concept is that it is best to plant species native to your region in a wildlife garden. They have a proven track record, because they are the plants with which birds, butterflies, and other native animals have coevolved and survived over the millennia.

What Is a Native Plant?

A native plant is a species that occurs naturally in a region and/or habitat without direct or indirect human intervention. A plant endemic to Europe and introduced to North America is not native to this continent. Likewise, a plant native to one region of North America is not native to another region unless it originated there without our help.

Ecologically speaking, political boundaries such as national or state lines have no bearing on plant distribution. Plant ecologists have divided North America into a number of plant provinces. The species in these distinct vegetation regions are deter-

Monarch butterflies depend on native milkweeds like this butterfly weed for their survival because milkweeds are the exclusive food source for their caterpillars, shown here.

mined by such factors as high and low temperatures in summer and winter, or total annual precipitation. More information on native species groupings and how to use them in a garden setting can be found on Brooklyn Botanic Garden's website (bbg.org/wildlife).

What Is Cross-Pollination?

Cross-pollination is the transfer of pollen from the flower of one plant to the flower of another individual to fertilize it. Often this is accomplished by an insect or other animal pollinator. Many species require cross-pollination to set seed or for genetic health. This means you need to plant at least two and preferably more individuals of the same species. Some plants, called dioecious species, have separate male and female plants, which means you should plant at least one male and one female plant to promote cross-pollination and the resulting production of the fruits on which birds and other wildlife depend. Hollies (*Ilex* species), willows (*Salix* species), and eastern red cedar (*Juniperus virginiana*) are examples of dioecious plants.

Bird Gardens

If you love birds, and who doesn't—bird feeding and bird watching are two of the most popular pastimes in both the United States and Canada—you can do a lot for them, right in your own backyard, beyond setting out seeds and a birdbath. By diversifying the vegetation in your yard to provide resting and nesting places and foods during all seasons, you can attract a lot of bird species in addition to the jays, cardinals, and other frequent visitors to suburban and city gardens.

On the pages that follow, you'll find lots of useful tips for creating a great, all-purpose bird garden no matter how small or large your yard. For more specialized plantings you'll find additional information in subsequent chapters. For example, if you live along one of the major flyways, you can help declining songbird populations by creating a bed-and-breakfast for weary warblers and other long-distance migrants (see "Stopover Gardens," page 26). All animal-friendly borders, even prairie landscapes, include a few evergreen shrubs for protection from predators and stormy weather; see the chapter on creating evergreen bird refuges for details (page 38). No garden is complete without hummingbirds darting from bloom to bloom, and there is an entire chapter devoted to them and their favorite flowers (see page 72).

Birds and other wildlife require water to survive. Here, an Oak Titmouse sips water at a birdbath.

Many trees and shrubs produce fruits just the right size to pass through the gape of a bird, like this Bohemian Waxwing.

Birds and Plants—A Mutual Attraction

Cole Porter could have been teaching Botany 101 when he wrote "Let's Do It," one of the catchiest songs of all time. The lyrics go something like this: When the little bluebird starts to sing "Spring," when the little bluebell starts to ring "Ding, dong, ding," it's just nature doing its thing. "Birds do it, bees do it…" I can hear Satchmo croon.

Botanists may be a bit less poetic, but they're saying essentially the same thing when they expound upon the intimate relationship between birds and plants. Plants get decked out in colorful foliage and flowers to attract the birds and other creatures that are their sexual intermediaries. In return for a yummy meal of fruit or nectar, the birds pollinate the plants and disperse their seeds across the landscape.

It's estimated that in the eastern deciduous forests alone, at least 300 trees, shrubs, and vines depend solely on birds to spread their seeds far and wide. Other animals, like rodents, destroy seeds by gnawing through the seed coat, but birds eat only the fleshy outer part of the fruit. Although the seeds remain intact as they pass through the birds' gizzards, their protective seed coat is scarified, or scratched, improving the chances of germination.

Following are a few of the ways that the mutual love affair between birds and plants is manifested in the wild and in the garden.

- Plants that depend on birds to fertilize their flowers often bear blooms with shapes that are tailor-made for the size and curve of the particular pollinator's bill.

- Plants that depend on birds to disperse their seeds produce brightly colored fruits— no coincidence, because most seed-eating birds have a great eye for color.

- Most trees and shrubs bear small fruits, no more than three-fifths of an inch in diameter—just small enough to pass through a bird's gape.

- Some plant or other is always in fruit, providing food for birds in all seasons. But the fruiting reaches a crescendo precisely when migration reaches its peak and huge numbers of birds desperately need energy for their marathon journeys.

The Hazards of Nonnative Plants

We gardeners should be careful not to come between native birds and their partners, native plants. We've planted a number of nonnative species that are invading and degrading the wild habitats upon which birds depend. For example, Japanese honeysuckle (*Lonicera japonica*) has aggressively formed monocultures across the U.S., and although birds readily consume its fruits, it is replacing once-diverse native food sources, including dogwoods and viburnums, limiting the nutritious variety of foods that were historically available throughout the year. A good rule of thumb is never to grow a nonnative plant with fruits that are dispersed by birds, because they invariably will be scattered throughout the landscape, with possibly deleterious effects.

Originally introduced as a pretty garden plant, Japanese honeysuckle vine easily escaped into the wild, aided by birds that readily consume its fruits and then distribute its seeds.

Natural Foods for Wild Birds

Seven types of plants are important sources of bird food. By including a few of each in your garden you will provide a smorgasbord that will attract the widest variety of birds in all seasons.

Summer-Fruiting Trees and Shrubs

This category includes wild cherries, mulberries, blackberries, blueberries, raspberries, plums, and elderberries. Among the birds that can be attracted by these plants are thrashers, catbirds, thrushes, waxwings, cardinals, towhees, vireos, tanagers, and grosbeaks.

Fall-Fruiting Plants

Shrubs and vines whose fruits are ripe in autumn are important both for long-distance travelers, which build up fat reserves prior to and during migration, and for nonmigratory species that must enter the winter season in good physical condition. Fall-fruiting plants include dogwoods and viburnums.

Winter Fruits and Spring Leftovers

Fruits of these species remain on the plants long after they first ripen. In fact, many are not palatable until they have frozen and thawed numerous times. Examples are bayberry, snowberry, sumacs, and Virginia creeper. These plants help overwintering birds get through the season and are popular with early arrivals such as robins, catbirds, and wrens.

Acorn and Other Nut Plants

These include oaks, hickories, buckeyes, and hazels. While their supersize seeds are still on the trees, only birds with beaks big and strong enough to pluck them off and crack their shells can eat them, including woodpeckers, crows, and jays. Once the nuts fall to the ground, they are consumed by a smattering of large birds like turkeys, and any stray bits of the meat are gobbled up by a variety of smaller birds, including wrens.

Conifers

Conifers—evergreen trees and shrubs that include pines, spruces, firs, arborvitae, junipers, and cedars— are important as escape cover, resting places, winter shelter, and summer nesting sites. Some also provide birds with sap, buds, and seeds.

Grasses and Legumes

Grasses and legumes provide cover for ground-nesting birds—especially if the area is not mowed during the nesting season. Some grasses and legumes provide seeds as well. During autumn, migrating birds will feast on the fresh crop of seeds. If you delay cutting back the dead flower heads, flocks of birds, including Common Redpolls, White-throated Sparrows, and finches, will finish off any stray seeds still on the plants in winter.

Nectar-Producing Plants

Nectar-producing trees, shrubs, vines, and wildflowers are important food sources for hummingbirds, and orioles sometimes sip the stuff too. Orioles drink nectar from the cuplike blooms of tulip trees; hummingbirds are most attracted by flowers with tubular red corollas.

Think bird food: Juniper (left), flowering dogwood, red oak, grasses, trumpet honeysuckle.

Ten Steps to a Bird Garden

Whether you have an established yard or are starting from scratch, following are ten general guidelines that will help you create a garden with maximum appeal for both people and birds.

1. **Re-create the layers of plant growth found in local woodlands—canopy, understory, shrub, and ground layer.** By re-creating all these various layers, you maximize value to wildlife. In general, the more distinctive vertical strata there are, the more diverse the plant life, and therefore the more habitats created for a more diverse array of animal life.

   In deciduous forests of the mid-Atlantic, for example, dominant trees such as oaks form a high canopy above smaller trees such as flowering dogwoods and serviceberries. Below this is a layer of tall and shorter shrubs such as viburnums and blueberries, and finally groundcovers such as wild sarsaparilla and ferns. The layers are intertwined by vines such as wild grapes and Virginia creeper.

Birds use all these layers. Wood Thrushes and vireos, for example, usually sing from the canopy trees. Titmice feed in the flowering dogwood, and cardinals nest and rest in the tall shrubs. Robins, meanwhile, scratch around in the leaf litter for worms, pillbugs, and other treats.

If you have a shade tree or two on your property, you have a head start on a great bird garden; just fill in around them with smaller trees, shrubs, and wildflowers—these are the layers most used by birds yet most often missing from the typical suburban landscape. If you have no trees, consider planting a few, or grow a variety of fruiting shrubs and brambles that many birds love. If you live in the Midwestern or Plains states, plant native wildflowers and grasses with a few scattered shrubs for perching and cover.

2. **Select plants so that there is food for birds in all seasons.** See "Natural Foods for Wild Birds," page 12, for details.

3. **Plant small trees and shrubs, including hollies, in same-species clumps to boost cross-pollination and fruit production.** This will also benefit birds by advertising massed displays of fruit.

4. **Plant some conifers and broadleaf evergreens, which birds use for cover during storms.** Conifers are also preferred resting and nesting sites. See page 40 for details on how to create evergreen bird refuges in your yard.

5. **Leave a dead tree for birds to perch on or to use as a singing post.** Woodpeckers will carve out nesting cavities in it and use it for drumming, which they employ instead of songs to keep competitors out of their territory.

6. **Plant vines or allow wild ones to grow.** Many provide abundant fruits, and almost all make good perching and nesting places.

Vertical vegetation layers (left) create habitat where many different birds find cover, food, and places for resting and nesting. A large conifer (right) is a useful shelter, especially in inclement weather.

7. **Supply a source of water, which birds need not only for drinking but also for bathing or just cooling off on a hot summer day.** Hummingbirds are small enough to bathe in a few drops of water that collect on leaves, but most land birds prefer to drink or bathe in shallow puddles, pools, or ponds. They'll also drink and splash in a birdbath. See page 88 for information on how to create easy water features for wildlife.

8. **Provide nest boxes, which are a good substitute for increasingly scarce natural tree cavities.** At least 48 species are known to rear their families in prefab or homemade birdhouses, from bluebirds to warblers. See page 103 for information on which species use them and what their requirements are.

9. **Leave lots of leaf litter under trees and shrubs for ground-feeding birds.** It's a great excuse to be lazy, and it's a lot friendlier to wildlife than the typical suburban lawn. Robins, towhees, juncos, and native sparrows are just a few of the species that pick through this natural leaf mulch in search of the worms, insects, and spiders that live there.

10. **Don't use pesticides.** Some of them harm birds directly, and others contaminate the insects and other creatures that birds eat.

Clusters of the same type of fruiting plants, such as these hollies and sumacs, signal an abundant supply of food to hungry birds and also help with cross-pollination and fruit set.

The Vertical Layers of a Forest

Forests consist of several different layers of vegetation. The topmost layer is the canopy, formed by the tallest trees. Below the canopy there are as many as three more distinct layers of mostly shade-loving vegetation. Just below the canopy is the understory of smaller trees, such as flowering dogwoods. Below the understory is the shrub layer, which consists of both shrubs and young trees. Ferns, wildflowers, mosses, and other plants compose the tapestry known as the ground layer. Birds use all these layers for perching, resting, nesting, and foraging. Emulate nature in your garden by creating layers of wildlife-friendly species.

Low-bush blueberries grow naturally in acidic soils in open woodlands and sunny fields, where they may spread to form large colonies.

Bird Plants for Your Region

NORTHEAST

Trees

Acer saccharum, sugar maple
Amelanchier stolonifera,
   running serviceberry
Betula lenta, sweet birch
Prunus serotina, black cherry
Quercus alba, white oak

Shrubs

Gaylussacia baccata, black huckleberry
Myrica pennsylvanica, Northern bayberry
Rubus species, blackberries
   and raspberries
Vaccinium angustifolium,
   lowbush blueberry
Viburnum recognitum,
   northern arrowwood

Vines

Celastrus scandens, American
   bittersweet (not the invasive
   nonnative *C. orbiculatus*,
   oriental bittersweet)

SOUTHEAST

Trees

Betula nigra, river birch
Carya species, hickories
Morus rubra, red mulberry
Quercus laevis, turkey oak
Quercus virginiana, live oak

Shrubs

Prunus angustifolia, Chickasaw plum
Rhus copallina, winged sumac
Rosa palustris, swamp rose
Vaccinium corymbosum,
   highbush blueberry
Viburnum obovatum, Walter's viburnum

Vines

Parthenocissus quinquefolia,
   Virginia creeper

FLORIDA

Trees

Celtis laevigata, sugarberry
Diospyros virginiana,
   American persimmon
Fraxinus carolina, pop ash
Quercus chapmanii, Chapman's oak
Sabal palmetto, cabbage palm

Shrubs

Ardisia escallonoides, marlberry
Eugenia species, stoppers
Forestiera segregata, Florida privet
Myrica cerifera, wax myrtle
Persea borbonia, redbay

Vines

Ipomoea pes-caprae, railroad vine

Left: Northeastern native black cherry
Right: Southeastern native Virginia creeper

Bird Plants for Your Region, continued

CENTRAL PRAIRIES AND PLAINS

Trees
Carya illinoensis, pecan
Celtis occidentalis, common hackberry
Fraxinus pennsylvanica, green ash
Prunus mexicana, Mexican plum
Quercus macrocarpa, bur oak

Shrubs
Rhus species, sumacs
Ribes missouriense,
   Missouri gooseberry
Rosa arkansana, prairie rose
Viburnum prunifolium, blackhaw
Viburnum opulus var. *americanum*,
   American cranberrybush
   (not the invasive nonnative *V. opulus* var.
   opulus, European cranberrybush)

Vines
Parthenocissus vitacea, woodbine

SOUTHWEST

Trees
Amelanchier utahensis,
   Utah serviceberry
Cercidium microphyllum, little leaf
   palo verde
Chilopsis linearis, desert willow
Parkinsonia aculeata, horsebean
   palo verde
Prunus emarginata, bitter cherry

Shrubs
Acacia greggii, catclaw
Calliandra eriophylla, fairy duster
Celtis pallida, desert hackberry
Ribes cereum, wax currant
Salix lasiolepis, arroyo willow

Vines
Clematis ligusticifolia, western
   white clematis

Southwestern native bitter cherry

California native green manzanita

CALIFORNIA

Trees
Arbutus menziesii, Pacific madrone
Cercis occidentalis, western redbud
Quercus agrifolia, coast live oak
Sorbus californica, California
  mountain ash
Washingtonia filifera, California
  fan palm

Shrubs
Adenostoma fasciculatum, chamise
Arctostaphylos species, manzanitas
Artemisia californica, sagebrush
Cornus glabrata, brown-twig dogwood
Prunus ilicifolia, hollyleaf cherry

Vines
Lonicera hispidula, California
  honeysuckle

NORTHWEST

Trees
Acer macrophyllum, bigleaf maple
Crataegus douglasii, western hawthorn
Fraxinus latifolia, Oregon ash
Malus fusca, Oregon crabapple
Quercus garryana, Oregon white oak

Shrubs
Mahonia aquifolium, Oregon grape
Gaultheria shallon, salal
Frangula (*Rhamnus*) *purshiana*,
  cascara buckthorn
Rubus parviflorus, thimbleberry
Salix lucida subsp. *caudata*,
  Pacific willow

Vines
Lonicera ciliosa, trumpet honeysuckle

A catbird feeds on bunches of grapes.

BIRD FEEDING:
Questions and Answers

No wildlife garden is complete without some feeders. According to the National Audubon Society, nearly one-third of the adult population in the U.S. and Canada feeds birds, using about a billion pounds of birdseed each year as well as tons of suet. Here are the answers to some common questions about feeding birds in your backyard.

Q: Do bird feeders help or hurt birds?

A: Scientists haven't been knocking down funders' doors to support studies of this issue, but research so far suggests that backyard feeders aren't creating helpless populations of dependent wintering birds, preventing birds from migrating, or transforming birds into slackers that become addicted to the easy life and forget how to hunt and forage. That's not to say that birds don't flock to feeders during cold weather—not surprising, since feeders reduce the time it takes them to find food, and it's much easier to pluck a sunflower seed from a feeder than to pry a hibernating insect out of bark. However, feeding birds certainly is not as helpful as creating garden habitat, which provides places to hide, rest, and nest, in addition to food for a greater variety of birds.

Q: Can birds catch diseases at feeders?

A: Yes, which is why it's extremely important to disinfect them once or twice a month by immersing the feeders in a nine-to-one water-to-bleach solution, then rinsing them thoroughly. For tips on cleaning hummingbird feeders, see page 75.

Q: How can I keep hawks and other predators from picking off my backyard birds?

A: If a hawk or other raptor shows up regularly to dine on the songbirds congregating at your feeders, stop feeding long enough for the small birds to disperse and the predators to become resigned to having to hunt elsewhere. And keep in mind that domestic cats account for about 30 percent of all birds killed at feeders. They're such stealthy hunters that they can stalk and pounce without jingling the bells on their collars. So keep your cats indoors and let them watch the birds with you through the window.

Q: How can I stop birds from crashing into my windows?

A: According to a recent study, this is the most common cause of death associated with backyard feeders, accounting for one to ten deaths per building a year. To prevent collisions, stretch fruit-tree netting taut several inches in front of the glass.

Q: Will birds get stuck to metal feeder perches when temperatures are below freezing?

A: In a word, no. A bird's feet are covered with dry scales, so there is no moisture that could freeze and adhere the bird to frigid feeder parts.

Q: How can I keep squirrels off my feeders?

A: It isn't easy, but the best way to foil squirrels is to hang feeders not from trees or eaves but rather poles at least five feet off the ground and as far as possible from your house and nearby trees and shrubs—squirrels can leap as far as six feet! And attach to the pole either an inverted cone at least 13 inches in diameter or a special squirrel-deterring dish 15 inches in diameter. Then keep your fingers crossed.

FIVE FEEDERS EVERY YARD SHOULD HAVE

You'll attract the widest variety of bird species if you provide different types of feeders. Each type caters to different kinds of birds that typically feed at different heights. The following five feeder types will attract a delightful assortment of birds to your yard. See page 75 for information on hummingbird feeders.

1. Tube Feeder for Sunflower Seeds

If you can have only a single feeder, this is the one. Hang it on a branch or pole at least five feet off the ground. Select a model with metal ports so that squirrels and house sparrows will not be able to gnaw on the holes.

2. Tube Feeder for Thistle Seeds

Especially designed to dispense thistle seeds, also known as niger seeds, these tubes have smaller holes to accommodate the thinner seeds and smaller-beaked birds that eat them, including goldfinches, redpolls, and Pine Siskins.

3. Suet Feeder

The most durable are cages in which the suet cakes are placed. Suet is eaten readily by woodpeckers, chickadees, titmice, and nuthatches, and occasionally by wrens, warblers, and creepers.

4. Ground-Feeding Table

The best models are screen-bottomed trays that sit several inches off the ground.

Some have covers to help shield the seed from rain and snow; others are surrounded by wire mesh to keep out squirrels and crows and other large birds.

5. Hopper Feeder

A hopper can store several pounds of seed and dispense it on demand while protecting it from the elements. Mount it on a pole about five feet off the ground and it'll attract all the birds that come to tube feeders as well as cardinals, jays, and other larger birds.

Goldfinches and other small-beaked birds flock to thistle feeders.

FIVE FOODS FOR FEATHERED FRIENDS

Some seed mixes are bulked up with agricultural products like wheat and oats, which most birds discard in favor of their preferred foods. Many blends also include cracked corn, which is nearly as popular with ground-feeding birds as millet but is susceptible to rot. To get the greatest bang for your buck, provide the following:

1. Sunflower Seed

There are two major types: Black-oil sunflower seed is the preferred seed of most small birds, including chickadees and titmice. Striped sunflower seed is another favorite, but get it hulled to appeal to the widest variety of birds, including evening and pine grosbeaks.

2. Thistle Seed

The preferred food of American Goldfinches, Lesser Goldfinches, and Common Redpolls, these seeds do not come from common thistles but rather a tropical shrub, so you won't be adding to the weed population by offering them to feathered friends. They're sometimes called "black gold" because they're relatively pricey, but they're full of nutritious oil and are a great source of energy.

3. Suet

This fat-based treat sometimes includes seeds and/or chopped dried fruit, cracker crumbs, or other foods and is available in blocks to fit suet feeders. It attracts many insect-eating birds, including woodpeckers, kinglets, Bushtits, and Brown Creepers.

4. Millet

White millet is ambrosia for ground-feeding birds with small beaks, such as juncos, sparrows, and quail. They'll also pick at red millet but like it less.

5. Fresh Fruit

In spring, set out fruit to attract orioles, tanagers, and grosbeaks, including orange halves, apricots, cherries, and grapes.

Favorite bird foods: sunflower, millet, and thistle seeds

Stopover Gardens for Migrating Songbirds

Every spring millions of migrating songbirds fly 600 miles or more from the Yucatán Peninsula clear across the Gulf of Mexico. They proceed in waves up through the East, Midwest, and Plains states. Many continue to the vast coniferous forests of Canada, or as far north as the Arctic. Species that breed in the western states may have to fly for hours over inhospitable terrain in Mexico's Chihuahuan Desert before they can find refuge in the relatively lush vegetation of bosques along the middle Rio Grande. In fall, migrating songbirds make the same grueling trip in reverse. The rigors of these migrations leave them in unfamiliar landscapes when they're close to their physiological limits.

Since the 1950s these biannual migratory marathons have become even more of a challenge: Vast stretches of natural habitat along North America's major flyways have been carved up and developed, contributing to the decline of some songbird species. If high-quality habitat is not available, exhausted and emaciated migratory birds must continue until they find adequate food and cover. If they're too thin or weak to continue, they'll either starve or succumb to predators or harsh weather.

On the pages that follow, you'll learn how to transform your garden into a rest stop for weary migrants. If you live east of the Mississippi, you can create a songbird hedge or hedgerow. In the West, vegetation along streamsides and marshes can be restored with floodplain terraces planted with native trees and shrubs to provide stopover habitat along flyways.

The map shows the four major North American migration flyways used by millions of songbirds each year. In spring migrating birds fly 600 miles or more from their southern wintering grounds to their breeding grounds up north. In fall they make the exhausting trip in reverse.

North American Migration Flyways

Atlantic Flyway
Mississippi Flyway
Central Flyway
Pacific Flyway

During its voyage south in fall, a migrating Wood Thrush feeds on wax myrtle berries.

Bed-and-Breakfast for Weary Songbirds

The scattered trees and turf typical of the suburban landscape may provide useful habitat for blue jays, cardinals, and others, but to ease the plight of warblers, vireos, thrushes, and other threatened migratory songbirds, we have to transform our gardens into stopover habitats. The vast majority of migrating songbirds fly by night. These nocturnal travelers, including warblers, vireos, thrushes, and sparrows, leave their daytime hangouts just after dusk and spend the next eight to ten hours flying. Near dawn they descend and must find places to feed and rest until, in a day or two, they are strong enough to continue their journey.

In our gardens, we can make life easier for avian migrants by providing areas with as many of the different layers of plants found in a healthy forest as possible: the tallest trees that form its roof, smaller understory trees, shrubs, and groundcovers. Vines often connect the various layers, clambering up bushes and high into the trees. The goal is to re-create the gamut of habitat niches preferred by different species. For example, the Mourning Warbler has a definite affinity for shrubby thickets, whereas the Magnolia Warbler favors both tall and understory trees. Two-thirds of all the migrants observed in one study were found in shrubs and understory trees—the layers most often missing in the typical suburban landscape.

Berries and Blooms

Native shrubs loaded with berries are magnets for migrating songbirds, especially those heading south for the winter. To ensure that they reach either their breeding or wintering grounds, migrants must put on enormous amounts of fat. A Blackpoll Warbler, for example, which breeds in Canada, can almost double its weight, ballooning from about 12 grams (half an ounce) to more than 20 grams. The extra fat makes it possible for the tiny bird to fly nonstop between the New England coast and the northern coast of South America. But most songbirds can't accumulate enough fat to make their trips in one continuous flight; they depend on finding suitable stopover habitats, places with an abundant supply of emerging insects in spring and fruits and bugs in fall. Hummingbirds look for both bugs and nectar from tube-shaped flowers.

Songbirds at Risk

The U.S. Fish and Wildlife Service considers 11 of the 96 neotropical songbird species, about 12 percent, as imperiled, and says the populations of another 68 percent have been declining. Some have declined dramatically—for example, Cerulean Warbler and Painted Bunting populations have plummeted 60 to 75 percent over the past three decades.

Scientists who study songbird population declines have devoted most of their time to investigating losses of nesting and winter habitat. Until quite recently, stopover habitat received scant attention. According to the small but growing cadre of stopover ecologists, large, unbroken tracts of natural habitat are best, but even small patches of stopover habitat in the middle of urban and agricultural areas can provide shelter and nourishment for famished songbirds.

Populations of the Cerulean Warbler have plummeted in recent years.

A Stopover Garden for the East, Midwest, and Plains States

Studies have demonstrated that hedgerows—long, linear plantings of trees and shrubs first promoted in the mid-1930s to reduce soil erosion—are important stopover habitats in the Plains states. As recently as 60 years ago, fields and pastures bordered by hedgerows dominated the landscape in the eastern two-thirds of the country. Mature hedgerows typically included some canopy species, along with beautiful understory trees and shrubs such as native viburnums. Songbirds flourished in this environment.

If you live in the Northeast, Southeast, Midwest, or Plains states, whether your property is a small suburban lot or a vast estate, you can use the hedgerow as the model for your stopover garden. Concentrate on creating as many of the vertical layers as possible. If your property is small, leave out the largest trees and choose the more compact varieties of understory trees and shrubs.

Biologically, "living fences" such as hedgerows and hedges are infinitely more valuable than the warrens of wooden stockade and plastic picket fences that have appeared in communities across the country.

Creating a Hedgerow

- Plant the center or tallest part first, with a few scattered oak, tulip, or other canopy trees; consider buying the more natural clumping forms rather than the standard single-trunked, shade-tree forms.

- On either side and among the taller species, plant flowering and evergreen understory trees—dogwoods are among the best.

- After all the trees are installed, fill in the gaps with shrubs—the more different types the better—and a vine or two. Many migrants are attracted to thickets, dense masses of fruiting shrubs, vines, briars, and brambles.

- Along the edges of your stopover garden, plant various shrubs that bear lots of fall fruit.

- In front of the shrubs, plant clumps of nectar-rich flowers for hummingbirds. And while you're at it, include some milkweeds and goldenrods, favored plants of migrating monarch butterflies.

- Use native trees and shrubs when possible, because they are genetically programmed to leaf out, bloom, and fruit at precisely the right time for the migrants with which they've coevolved.

- For specific plant recommendations, see the the pages that follow.

Hedgerow Habitat for Migratory Birds

In this example of a hedgerow planting, black and white oak form the tallest or canopy layer. Below these is an understory of sassafras and dogwood trees. Arrowwood, chokeberry, and elderberry compose the layer of heavily fruiting shrubs. The grapevine produces additional fruits while the silky dogwood, native honeysuckle vine, and the herbaceous wildflowers that make up the ground layer provide nectar for hummingbirds as well as butterflies.

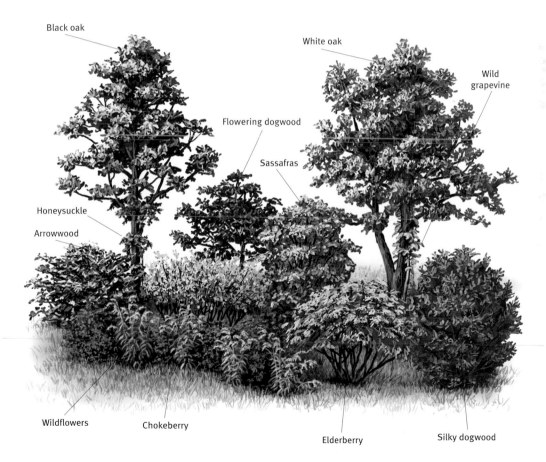

Black oak

White oak

Wild grapevine

Flowering dogwood

Sassafras

Honeysuckle

Arrowwood

Wildflowers

Chokeberry

Elderberry

Silky dogwood

Plants for the East, Midwest, and Plains States

Canopy trees

Liriodendron tulipifera, tulip tree
Magnolia grandiflora, southern magnolia
Magnolia virginiana, sweetbay magnolia
Nyssa sylvatica, black gum
Quercus species, oaks

Understory trees

Celtis occidentalis, hackberry
Cornus alternifolia, pagoda dogwood
Cornus amomum, silky dogwood
Cornus drummondii,
    rough-leaved dogwood
Cornus florida, flowering dogwood
Cornus racemosa, gray dogwood
Ilex cassine, dahoon holly
Ilex vomitoria, yaupon holly
Rhus typhina, staghorn sumac
Sassafras albidum, sassafras

Shrubs

Aronia arbutifolia, chokeberry
Ilex decidua, possumhaw holly
Ilex glabra, inkberry holly
Juniperus virginiana, eastern red cedar
Lindera benzoin, spicebush
Salix species, including coastal
    plain willow, *S. caroliniana*
Sambucus canadensis,
    American elderberry
Viburnum acerifolium,
    mapleleaf viburnum
Viburnum dentatum, arrowwood
Viburnum nudum, smooth witherod
Viburnum rufidulum, rusty haw

Vines

Celastrus scandens, American
    bittersweet (not to be confused with
    the invasive nonnative Oriental
    bittersweet, *C. orbiculatus*)
Parthenocissus quinquefolia,
    Virginia creeper
Vitis vulpina, wild grape

Gray dogwood (above) and chokeberry (facing page, top) form part of the fruiting layer of the stopover garden.

The fruits of chokeberry form late in the growing season and persist into winter.

Nectar plants for Ruby-throated Hummingbirds

Aquilegia canadensis, eastern columbine
Campsis radicans, trumpet creeper
Dicentra eximia, fringed bleeding heart
Heuchera americana, coral bells
Impatiens capensis, jewelweed
Lobelia cardinalis, cardinal flower

Lonicera sempervirens, coral honeysuckle (not to be confused with the invasive nonnative Japanese honeysuckle, *Lonicera japonica*)
Rhododendron viscosum, swamp azalea

The Tiniest Migrants

The tiniest of all migrating birds are hummingbirds. In spring, three-inch-long Ruby-throated Hummingbirds, which spend the winter as far south as Panama, begin the long flight across the Gulf of Mexico, making landfall in the southeastern states. Many continue up into southeastern Canada. Rufous Hummingbirds, which winter in Mexico, move through the Pacific lowlands to nest as far north as Alaska—farther north than any other hummer. For more on hummingbirds, see page 72.

A Ruby-throated Hummingbird probes for nectar in a columbine flower.

A Stopover Garden for the Western States

In the arid West, streamsides and washes are by far the most important habitats for migrating and breeding birds alike. Narrow green strips of woodland and shrubland, these floodplain habitats have a rich diversity of birds despite the arid setting. Yet more than 95 percent of this critical floodplain habitat in the western United States has been destroyed or degraded.

Spring floods create steplike terraces along streams, each with a distinctive type of vegetation and community of birds. The area closest to the stream, which is flooded each year, is built up and flattened by accumulating sediments the waters leave behind, forming the first terrace. Second and sometimes third terraces are created by occasional heavy floods. These terraces are drier and the vegetation is sparser.

Biologists compared migrants' use of large, continuous bands of streamside vegetation with their use of fragmented habitat islands (areas less than two and a half miles long) in southeastern Arizona. They found that migrating birds in need of rest and refueling used the isolated patches as much as the larger corridors, if not more. By restoring critical floodplains, gardeners and landowners can play a major role in the restoration of stopover habitat.

Restoring a Floodplain to Create Stopover Habitat

• Re-create the series of ascending zones or terraces found in these habitats; different species of birds use the different areas.

• Begin closest to the water with the first terrace. In undisturbed areas, this is usually covered with a tall, multilayered woodland of cottonwoods and willows frequented by Willow Flycatchers and Yellow Warblers, among other birds. Plant this zone densely with a mixture of trees and shrubs.

• As the ground rises, make the plantings looser and more scattered, as is typical of upland areas. Black-tailed Gnatcatchers and Lucy's Warblers are just two of the songbirds that frequent this type of open woodland. In the Southwest, mesquite, wolfberry, saltbush, and other plants that prefer drier soil grow on upper terraces.

- The particular assemblage of plant species varies somewhat by region and elevation, so look for those that are native to your area and situation. Try to use at least three different species, and ideally more than seven.

- For specific plant recommendations, see the the pages that follow.

Floodplain Habitat for Migratory Birds

In this example of a floodplain planting there are three steplike terraces. The first terrace includes canopy trees such as cottonwoods, along with understory trees and shrubs, including willows. These moisture-loving species form a dense, multilayered woodland. The two higher terraces are successively drier and the vegetation is sparser. In the Southwest, wolfberry, saltbush, and other shrubs that prefer drier soils grow on these upper terraces.

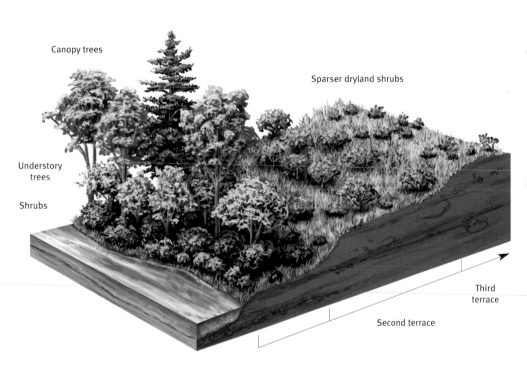

Canopy trees

Sparser dryland shrubs

Understory trees

Shrubs

Third terrace

Second terrace

First terrace

Wolfberry (above) and blue elderberry (facing page, top) are bird-friendly plant choices for the higher terraces of a floodplain planting.

Stopover Plants for the Western States

Canopy trees

Fraxinus latifolia, Oregon ash
Fraxinus velutina, Arizona ash
Juniperus deppeana, alligatorbark
    juniper
Pinus contorta, lodgepole pine
Pinus jeffreyi, Jeffrey pine
Pinus ponderosa, ponderosa pine
Platanus racemosa,
    California sycamore
Platanus wrightii, Arizona sycamore
Populus balsamifera, black cottonwood
Populus fremontii, Fremont cottonwood
Quercus lobata, valley oak

Understory trees

Celtis reticulata, netleaf hackberry
Prosopis pubescens,
    screwbean mesquite
Prosopis velutina, honey mesquite

Shrubs

Acer negundo, box elder
Alnus rhombifolia, white alder
Atriplex lentiformis, quailbush
Atriplex polycarpa, saltbush
Baccharis glutinosa, seep willow
Lycium species, wolfberries
Salix exigua, coyote willow
Salix goodingii, Gooding willow
Salix sessilifolia, sandbar willow
Sambucus caerulea, blue elderberry
Sambucus mexicana, Mexican elderberry
Symphoricarpos species, snowberries

Vines

Vitis arizonica, canyon grape
Vitis californica, California wild grape

Groundcover

Amorpha fruticosa, false indigo

Blue elderberry

Nectar plants for Rufous
Hummingbirds

Arbutus menziesii, Pacific madrone
Castilleja species, paintbrushes
Gaultheria shallon, salal
Ipomopsis aggregata, scarlet gilia

Lonicera involucrata, twinberry
Penstemon barbatus, scarlet bugler
Ribes sanguineum, flowering currant
Rubus spectabilis, salmonberry
Salvia greggii, autumn sage

Endangered Woodlands, Declining Songbirds

The floodplain woodlands of the arid West
are among the most imperiled habitats in
North America. In the 1600s, an estimated
4,800 acres of the floodplain of the lower
Colorado River were covered with Fremont
cottonwood; by 1900, only about 240 acres
remained. Only 29 acres of the once
extensive mature cottonwood-willow
woodland remain along the lower Rio
Grande. Along the rivers of the Sacramento
Valley, cottonwood-willow woodlands were
reduced from 775,000 acres to 12,000 acres by the 1970s. Many of the birds
they support, including migratory species like the endangered Willow
Flycatcher, have declined as the woodlands have disappeared.

Willow Flycatcher

Evergreen Refuges

All trees and shrubs provide cover, but none are better than evergreens, especially conifers, when birds need to beat a quick retreat. Evergreens also offer shelter from storms—even conifer needles, which may look flimsy, are very effective at shedding rain and snow and acting as windbreaks.

Birds that spend most of their time in the lower levels of a woodland often roost in smaller conifers, such as junipers. Pines and other large species offer shelter for far-ranging birds like crows and jays.

If you have a mature conifer on your property, it is probably already an inviting destination for birds. If you don't, a group of three or more young conifers will provide an attractive substitute. You can create visual appeal in your yard—and please feathered friends—by planting groups of conifers as hedges, to enclose garden rooms and other intimate spaces, or to hide and then reveal views along a path. If possible, scatter groups of evergreens so that they can function as "stepping stones," offering wildlife safe passage from one part of your property to the next.

Most conifers also make beautiful specimen trees. Some, such as the balsam fir, have the classic Christmas tree shape. Some, like the Colorado blue spruce, offer gorgeous foliage color. Others have attractive cones or bark, including the ponderosa pine, whose bark of irregular, yellow-brown plates is deeply furrowed.

As with other plants for wildlife, regionally native conifers are best, since they are more likely to host the native insects upon which birds depend. Natural forms, as opposed to contorted or other "improved" selections, typically provide the best bird habitat.

A Yellow-rumped Warbler feeds on juniper berries. In addition to providing food, evergreens also protect birds from predators and storms.

Some Conifers and the Birds That Use Them

Firs, *Abies* species

Native Habitat Firs are found throughout the West, the Northeast, upper Midwest, and some southern states.

Primary Attractions These densely branched trees provide an excellent source of cover for many birds. With age, they also produce a multitude of cones. Kinglets, Bushtits, chickadees, and other birds eat the insects on the foliage; titmice and nuthatches are among the birds that feed on the seeds.

Some Associated Birds In addition to the above, cardinals, jays, and many small birds nest or rest in firs.

Hemlocks, *Tsuga* species

Native Habitat Eastern and Carolina hemlocks are found in the East; mountain and western hemlocks are found in the Northwest, California, and Nevada.

Primary Attractions Hemlocks provide good cover during storms, night roosting spots for at least 22 species, and nesting places for forest warblers, among other birds. The seeds are a preferred winter food for chickadees, goldfinches, crossbills, and Pine Siskins.

Some Associated Birds In addition to the above, Northern Cardinals, Wood Thrushes, American Robins, nuthatches, titmice, tanagers, crows, jays utilize hemlocks.

Junipers, *Juniperus* species

Native Habitat Native junipers are found throughout the U.S. and Canada.

Primary Attractions Great cover is the primary virtue of these generally dense and prickly leafed conifers. Some species also produce huge crops of berrylike cones that are gobbled up by birds and prized as ornaments by people. For example, though Cedar Waxwings generally prefer deciduous trees, they get their name from eastern red cedar because of the way they wolf down the species' beautiful blue—and apparently tasty—cones. They're not alone; an estimated 45 other bird species dine on them too.

Some Associated Birds Cedar Waxwings, Brown Thrashers, Eastern Bluebirds, chickadees, titmice, kinglets, Tree Swallows, Yellow-rumped Warblers, Yellow-bellied Sapsuckers all enjoy the shelter and food provided by junipers.

Red Crossbills eat pine seeds as well as insects harboring in the bark of trees.

Spruces, *Picea* species

Native Habitat Spruces are found throughout the West, and in the upper Midwest, Northeast, and mid-Atlantic.

Primary Attractions Like other conifers, spruces are used for cover. The seeds in their cones are a source of food for some birds; other birds dine on the insects gleaned from the leaves and bark.

Some Associated Birds Colorado blue spruce alone provides seeds for a variety of mountain birds, including Scrub Jays, Steller's Jays, chickadees, grosbeaks, Pine Siskins, finches, and sparrows. Insects in the bark are relished by nuthatches, Brown Creepers, Nashville Warblers, and other warblers. The Olive-sided Flycatcher and other flycatchers perch in the branches.

Pines, *Pinus* species

Native Habitat Pines are found throughout the U.S.

Primary Attractions In addition to providing cover and roosting and nesting places, pines produce seeds in their cones and harbor insects under their bark. At least 48 species of birds are known to use the eastern white pine alone for feeding, resting, and nesting.

Some Associated Birds Wild Turkeys, woodpeckers, nuthatches, Brown Creepers, Pine Warblers, grosbeaks, tanagers, kinglets, Pine Siskins, and Red Crossbills are among the birds that eat the seeds or insects harbored in the bark. Raptors, including the Great Horned Owl, Screech Owl, and Pygmy Owl, roost and nest in pines.

Evergreens for Your Region

NORTHEAST

Abies balsamea, balsam fir
Picea glauca, white spruce
Pinus strobus, white pine
Thuja occidentalis, eastern arbovitae
Tsuga canadensis, eastern hemlock

SOUTHEAST

Ilex opaca, American holly
Juniperus silicicola, southern red cedar
Pinus palustris, longleaf pine
Pinus taeda, loblolly pine
Taxodium distichum, bald cypress

FLORIDA

Chrysophyllum oliviforme, satinleaf
Coccoloba diversifolia, pigeon plum
Jacquinia keyensis, joewood
Pinus elliotii var. *densa,* slash pine
Taxodium distichum var. *imbricarium,*
     pond cypress

CENTRAL PRAIRIES AND PLAINS

Juniperus ashei, Ashe juniper
Juniperus communis, common juniper
Juniperus scopulorum,
     Rocky Mountain juniper
Juniperus virginiana, eastern red cedar
Picea mariana, black spruce

Groups of evergreens or large mature specimens such as the white spruce (above) and Arizona cypress (left) offer birds safe passage from one part of your yard to the next.

SOUTHWEST

Cupressus arizonica, Arizona cypress
Juniperus deppeana, alligator juniper
Juniperus monosperma,
    oneseed juniper
Juniperus osteosperma, Utah juniper
Pinus monophylla, pinyon pine

CALIFORNIA

Abies concolor, white fir
Chamaecyparis lawsoniana,
    Port Orford cedar
Heteromeles arbutifolia, toyon
Pinus lambertina, sugar pine
Pinus sabiniana, digger pine

NORTHWEST

Calocedrus decurrens, incense cedar
Picea engelmannii, Engelmann spruce
Pinus contorta, shore pine
Pinus monticola, western white pine

Northwest native incense cedar

Flower Borders for Wildlife

Anyone who's looked at a gardening magazine in recent years knows that the art of creating beautiful flower borders has come of age in North America. But orchestrating these compositions of colorful blooms has been almost purely a question of aesthetics—of combining flowers in just the right shades of, say, gold and blue, and of placing the taller plants at the back of the border and the smaller ones in front. The lists of plants recommended for these borders are often heedless of the needs of birds, butterflies, and other creatures. In this chapter, you'll learn how to refine the conventional flower border to make it attractive not only to people but also to wildlife.

The Best Borders

• In most areas, mixed borders are best—vertically layered plantings that include small trees and shrubs, perennials, and annuals. In the Prairies and Plains states and provinces it's okay to leave out the trees, but it's still a good idea to include a shrub or two. Mixed borders are preferable because the various vertical layers create a variety of habitats for an array of different animals. Some birds perch or nest in the trees, others eat the berries provided by the shrubs. The flowering perennials provide nectar and other nourishment for butterflies, moths, hummingbirds, bats, and other pollinators. In the Central Prairies and Plains region, a herbaceous prairie-style border is ecologically appropriate as well.

Mixed borders that include small trees and shrubs as well as herbaceous perennials and annuals create diverse habitat for a variety of birds and other wildlife.

In this prairie border, clusters of nectar-rich native plants of the same species provide an abundance of food for birds, butterflies, and bees.

- Wildlife-friendly borders are inspired by local plant communities and are therefore most familiar and attractive to the creatures that live there year-round or pass through during spring and fall migration. In the East and Northwest, where deciduous and coniferous forests prevail, you can mimic the plant combinations found along woodland edges: small flowering trees such as dogwoods, viburnums and other shrubs, and native wildflowers like asters and goldenrods. Add annuals to provide even more color as well as nectar for pollinators. In the Midwest and Plains states, you can design a prairie-style border combining wildflowers such as coneflowers with bluestems and other native grasses and shrubby dogwoods and sumacs. If you live in an arid region, you can create architecturally striking combinations of native flowering trees, cacti, and spiky agaves and yuccas, softened by buckwheats, penstemons, and other wildflowers.

- Native trees, shrubs, and flowers are the backbone of these borders. They are the plants with which the local wildlife has evolved, which means they flower and produce the most nutritious fruits when the native wildlife need them most. A few nonnative flowers won't hurt, though. They provide nectar for many adult butterflies, which frequently aren't fussy about the sources of their sustenance. Many caterpillars, however, cannot survive without specific native trees, shrubs, and wildflowers. This is true for Monarchs, for example, whose larvae feed only on butterfly weed and other milkweeds (*Asclepias* species).

Building a Border

On the following pages, you'll find step-by-step instructions for two wildlife-friendly flower borders. The first example, a mixed border (page 48) incorporates woody plants as the foundation of the plan. The second example, a prairie border (page 50), focuses on grasses and a ready supply of native flowers in bloom from spring to fall. Following the two plans you'll find lists of regionally appropriate plants to mix and match: Small trees and shrubs (page 53), and herbaceous perennials and grasses that feed and shelter birds (page 55), bees (page 57), moths (page 59), bats (page 61) and—surprise!— beetles (page 63). To incorporate plants that attract hummingbirds and butterflies, see pages 72 and 80, respectively.

Wildlife-friendly flower borders emulate local plant communities and are therefore most familiar and attractive to the critters that live in your area.

How to Build a Mixed Border

This series of drawings depicts the three major steps in the development of a 6- by 12-foot section of a mixed border. The first step is choosing the woody plants that will anchor the border and provide a background hedge if appropriate. Step 2 is selecting the herbaceous perennials that will provide most of the flower color and nectar. In step 3, you add icing to the cake, selecting annuals that tie the border together and offer flowers throughout the growing season.

Step 1: Choose Small Trees and Shrubs

A hedge of inkberry (*Ilex glabra*) frames this woodland-edge border and provides a dense, fine-leafed evergreen background for the flowers and cover for birds. Inkberry grows 6 to 10 feet tall and produces shiny black fruits eaten by cardinals and bluebirds, among other birds. Sweet pepperbush (*Clethra alnifolia*) produces spikes of fragrant white or pink flowers that are bee and butterfly attractors.

Step 2: Choose Perennials

Perennials are the plants of choice for hungry pollinators and human flower lovers alike. To the right of the sweet pepperbush is a clump of anise hyssop (*Agastache foeniculum*), whose tall, 4- to 5-foot, bluish-purple flower spikes attract butterflies from midsummer to autumn. Directly in front of the shrub is New England aster (*Symphyotrichum novae-angliae*), and in the very front of the border is lower-growing eastern coneflower, (*Rudbeckia fulgida*) both favorites of butterflies, including the Monarch and American Lady.

Step 3: Add Annuals

Annuals offer both additional color and wildlife value. At the center of the border is flowering tobacco (*Nicotiana sylvestris*), with a cascade of pendant, fragrant white blooms with long, narrow floral tubes that are tailor-made for long-tongued hawkmoths. To the left of the coneflower is fragrant, deep purple heliotrope (*Heliotropium arborescens*), which caters to both butterflies and bees.

Plants Featured in This Border

SMALL TREES AND SHRUBS

Clethra alnifolia, sweet pepperbush
Ilex glabra, inkberry

ANNUAL FLOWERS

Heliotropium arborescens, heliotrope
Nicotiana sylvestris, flowering tobacco

PERENNIALS

Agastache foeniculum, anise hyssop
Rudbeckia fulgida, eastern coneflower
Symphyotrichum novae-angliae (syn. *Aster novae-angliae*), New England aster

The plants suggested here are just one possibility. See the lists of recommended plants on the pages that follow for choices appropriate to your climate and region.

How to Build a Prairie Border

This series of drawings depicts three major steps in the creation of a section of flower border roughly 13 by 5 feet comprised solely of herbaceous wildflowers and grasses native to the Prairie and Plains states. The first step is selecting the native grass or grasses that will anchor the border. Step 2 is choosing the largest wildflowers, the border's major focal points. Step 3 is selecting beautiful wildflowers that offer blooms throughout the growing season. The following 32-plant prairie border, irresistible to butterflies, was designed by Jennifer Baker of Prairie Nursery, in Westfield, Wisconsin.

Step 1: Choose Grasses

Grasses are the dominant plants in a prairie, the matrix in which the herbaceous wildflowers grow. Prairie dropseed (*Sporobolus heterolepis*), with its magnificent fountain of fine-textured, emerald-green leaves, is an elegant backdrop for the wildflowers in this border design.

Step 2: Select Large Wildflowers to Provide Focal Points

At the center of the border are single specimens of spectacular tall joe-pye weed (*Eutrochium fistulosum*), which can grow 5 to 8 feet tall, along with sweet joe-pye weed (*Eutrochium purpureum*) and ironweed (*Vernonia fasciculata*), which can reach 4 to 6 feet tall.

Step 3: Add Wildflowers for Continuous Bloom

From the spring flowers of eastern columbine (*Aquilegia canadensis*) and downy phlox (*Phlox pilosa*) to the autumn blooms of crooked-stem aster (*Symphiotrichum prenanthoides*), the border includes a variety of beautiful blooms to attract butterflies and hummingbirds from May through October.

Plants Featured in This Border

NATIVE GRASSES

Sporobolus heterolepis,
   prairie dropseed

SPRING FLOWERS

Aquilegia canadensis,
   eastern columbine
Phlox pilosa, downy phlox

EARLY-SUMMER FLOWERS

Asclepias tuberosa, butterfly weed
Asclepias sullivantii, Sullivant's
   milkweed

MIDSUMMER FLOWERS

Liatris pycnostachya, prairie blazingstar
Monarda fistulosa, bergamot
Vernonia fasciculata, ironweed

LATE-SUMMER FLOWERS

Eutrochium fistulosum (syn. *Eupatorium
   fistulosum*), tall joe-pye weed
Eutrochium purpureum (syn. *Eupatorium
   purpureum*), sweet joe-pye weed
Liatris spicata, dense blazingstar
Solidago ohioensis, Ohio goldenrod

FALL FLOWERS

Symphyotrichum prenanthoides (syn. *Aster
   prenanthoides*), crooked-stem aster

Even prairie borders benefit from a few trees and shrubs for perching and cover, either within the planting or nearby. See the lists of recommended evergreens on page 42 and small trees and shrubs on page 53.

Small Trees and Shrubs for Birds and Other Wildlife

Small trees and shrubs are the foundation of the wildlife border, as they are for any mixed border. They give the planting permanent structure, providing interest even in winter, when most herbaceous perennials have gone underground.

In a border designed to please not only people but also birds and other wildlife, there are additional considerations. A variety of woody plants provides different places to perch, hide, and nest, as well as nutritional foods during different seasons. In spring, serviceberries and other sweet fruits offer nourishment for hardworking parent birds. Fall migrants like thrushes require fatty fruits to fuel their long journeys; flowering dogwood is one of their favorites. Some fruits, like nannyberry, shrivel in place and help sustain wintering birds such as flickers. Other persistent fruits, including those of sumacs, are also important for early-spring migrants like bluebirds and thrashers.

The flowers of many woody plants, such as those of California lilac (*Ceanothus thyrsiflorus*), offer nectar to butterflies, bees, and other pollinators. Other trees

and shrubs, such as common spicebush, are host plants for caterpillars, including the Spicebush Swallowtail.

Use the lists on these pages and on pages 18–21, 32, 36, and 42 as a basis for a diverse selection of woody species that will nurture a variety of birds and other creatures in your garden. In return, the animals will pollinate the plants and disperse their seeds across the landscape.

Red currant is a hummingbird magnet in the Northwest.

Small Trees and Shrubs for Your Region

NORTHEAST

Amelanchier canadensis,
   shadbush, serviceberry
Cornus species (especially *C. florida*,
   C. racemosa), dogwoods
Gaylussacia baccata, black huckleberry
Ilex verticillata, winterberry
Lindera benzoin, common spicebush

SOUTHEAST

Cornus amomum, silky dogwood
Ilex species (including *I. cassine*,
   I. glabra, and *I. vomitoria*), hollies
Myrica cerifera, wax myrtle
Prunus caroliniana, Carolina
   cherry-laurel
Serenoa repens, saw palmetto

FLORIDA

Chrysobalanus icaco, cocoplum
Coccoloba uvifera, sea grape
Erythrina herbacea, coral bean
Lycium carolinianum, Christmas berry
Myrcianthes fragrans, Simpson stopper

CENTRAL PRAIRIES AND PLAINS

Amelanchier arborea,
   downy serviceberry
Cornus drummondii, rough-leafed
   dogwood
Corylus americana, hazelnut
Rhus species (including *R. glabra*,
   R. typhina), sumacs
Viburnum lentago, nannyberry

SOUTHWEST

Atriplex lentiformis, quailbush
Encelia farinosa, brittlebush
Larrea tridentata, creosote bush
Prosopis velutina, mesquite
Sambucus caerulea, blue elderberry

CALIFORNIA

Arctostaphylos species, manzanitas
Ceanothus species, California lilacs
Heteromeles arbutifolia, toyon
Myrica californica, Pacific wax myrtle
Ribes aureum, golden currant

NORTHWEST

Amelanchier alnifolia,
   western serviceberry
Cornus species (especially *C. nuttallii*,
   C. sericea), dogwoods
Mahonia nervosa, Oregon grape
Ribes sanguineum, red currant
Vaccinium parvifolium, red huckleberry,
   Utah serviceberry

**Insects are attracted to yaupon flowers;
birds and mammals eat the fruit of this
small evergreen holly.**

Bird Flowers and Grasses

The flowers of many herbaceous perennials produce seeds that are relished by birds in summer, fall, and if you delay deadheading, even winter. The stems of the taller plants make great perches for goldfinches and other songbirds. They also provide dense cover for birds and other wildlife.

Sunflowers are among the best bird flowers. For example, songbirds perch on the six-foot stems of the downy sunflower, *Helianthus mollis*. Its beautiful butter-yellow blooms appear in August, producing seeds that are goldfinch favorites. Another spectacular wildflower relished by birds is the cup plant, *Silphium perfoliatum*, which has it all—tall stems for perching and cover, nutritious seeds, and even water, which is trapped in the cups formed by the plant's large leaves and can last for days.

Native grasses offer both shelter and seed heads to nourish birds and also provide winter interest in the garden. (Both the grasses and the native perennials will continue to feed and shelter birds through the winter, so delay deadheading until spring.) In herbaceous borders, the grasses stand in for all the woody plants in a mixed border, anchoring the planting and providing a green backdrop for the colorful wildflower blooms.

The plants listed on the opposite page are some of the best native herbaceous plants for bird food and cover throughout the year. Combine the grasses and wildflowers to create a spectacular prairie or meadow border. For maximum value for your feathered friends, be sure to add a birdbath or another source of water (see page 90). See page 78 for favorite hummingbird flowers.

Birds are fond of the seeds of yellow coneflower.

Indian grass is appreciated by birds for its seeds and as nesting material.

Bird Flowers and Grasses

WILDFLOWERS

Cassia bebecarpa, wild senna
Helianthus mollis, downy sunflower
Helianthus occidentalis,
   western sunflower
Helianthus strumosus,
   woodland sunflower
Liatris species, blazingstars
Ratibida pinnata, yellow coneflower
Rudbeckia subtomentosa,
   sweet black-eyed susan
Silphium perfoliatum, cup plant
Solidago rigida, stiff goldenrod

GRASSES

Bouteloua curtipendula,
   sideoats grama
Panicum virgatum, switchgrass
Schizachyrium scoparium,
   little bluestem
Sorghastrum nutans, Indian grass
Sporobolus heterolepis,
   prairie dropseed

Lupines are some of the wildflowers favored by North American native bees and bumblebees.

Bee Flowers

On lazy summer days it's fun to go out in the garden, flop down on an old chaise longue, sip a margarita, and watch pollinators at work on the flowers. While butterflies are the divas of these botanical lovefests, flitting from bloom to bloom, bees are the workaholics, diligent and dependable.

Bees are also the cupids of the plant world. They fertilize most of our favorite flowers and pollinate a third of the plants we eat. They're also the exclusive pollinators of several imperiled wildflowers, including native monkshoods and lady's tresses orchids.

Bees are in trouble. In recent years parasitic mites and a mysterious malady known as CCD (colony collapse disorder) have killed large numbers of nonnative honeybees. Meanwhile, the natural habitats of native bees have continued to be degraded and destroyed. Among the native pollinating bees are chubby bumblebees with striped fur coats, as well as so-called solitary bees that don't live in hives, such as carpenter bees (which look a lot like bumblebees but have a shiny black rear end), mason bees, and digger bees.

Fortunately, we can help improve the lot of native bees by planting the flowers they love, whether we garden on an acre or in a window box. Just provide a steady food supply by growing favorite bee plants that bloom in all the seasons bees are active. It also helps to provide some nesting sites, including brush piles, clumps of moss, or even prefabricated bumblebee nest boxes (see page 111).

ANATOMY OF A BEE FLOWER

- Bees don't see red, but they do see yellow, blue, and ultraviolet hues. Thus the blooms they prefer are mostly yellow or blue, with UV nectar guides—bizarre wavy lines or leopardlike spots on their petals that guide the bees into the flower.

- Bees have good noses, and the flowers they pollinate usually have a delicate, sweet scent.

- Bee blooms usually have a small, narrow floral tube that suits the tongue length of the bee species that evolved with it.

- Some flowers are particularly suited for pollination by bumblebees. Modified lower petals serve as sturdy landing pads. Flowers like monkshoods will open only if the bee is hefty enough to pop open its petals.

A bumblebee probes for nectar in an aster's yellow disk flowers.

Bee Flowers

NATIVE TREES AND SHRUBS

Aloysia gratissima, bee brush
Arctostaphylos species, manzanitas
Ceanothus thyrsiflorus, California lilac
Cephalanthes occidentalis, buttonbush
Chilopsis linearis, desert willow
Clethra alnifolia, sweet pepperbush
Cornus species, dogwoods
Sambucus species, elderberries
Vaccinium species, blueberries
Viburnum species (especially *V. dentatum*, *V. cassinoides*, *V. lentago*), viburnums

NATIVE WILDFLOWERS

Aconitum species, monkshoods
Eurybia and *Symphyotrichum* (*Aster*) species, asters
Dalea species, Indigo bushes
Eriogonum species, buckwheats
Lobelia siphilitica, great blue lobelia
Liatris species, blazingstars

Lupinus species, lupines
Mertensia pulmonarioides, Virginia bluebells
Penstemon species, Penstemons
Phacelia species, phacelias
Salvia species (especially *S. azurea*, *S. clevelandi*, *S. farinacea*), salvias

HERBS

Agastache foeniculum, anise hyssop
Borago officinalis, borage
Origanum majorana, marjoram
Origanum × majoricum, Italian oregano
Rosmarinus officinalis, rosemary

NONNATIVE ANNUALS AND PERENNIALS

Antirrhinum majus, snapdragon (especially old-fashioned single-flowered varieties)
Lavandula species, lavenders
Nepeta species, catmints, catnips
Perovskia atriplicifolia, Russian sage
Veronica spicata, speedwell

Adult Luna Moths lack mouthparts and cannot feed. Lure them to your yard by growing the plants favored by their caterpillars.

Moth Flowers

Butterflies account for only a small percentage of the species in the order Lepidoptera. The remainder are moths. These poor creatures have gotten a bum rap—only a tiny fraction eat their way through prized plants or priceless woolens.

It's true that most moths are small, mousy-brown jobs, but some have spots, bands of color, and graceful shapes to rival those of any butterfly. Like butterflies, moths go through a metamorphosis of several stages, the most familiar being the caterpillar and the adult. And like adult butterflies, most adult moths sip nectar from flowers.

Among the most fascinating nectar-sipping moths are the hawk or sphinx moths, some of the fastest fliers of the lepidopteran world. The wings of the adults are narrow and often showy, and their bodies are stout but streamlined, tapering to a point.

Some of the most ravishing species are the giant silk moths, including the Cecropia, Polyphemus, Promethea, and Luna, among North America's largest night-flying insects. Ranging from browns to bright oranges to luminous greens, their wings are accented by bright "eyespots." The adults lack mouthparts and cannot feed, so they live only a few days; however, you can lure them to your yard by growing the plants favored by their caterpillars.

ANATOMY OF A MOTH FLOWER

- Night-flying moths pollinate white or pale-colored flowers that are visible at night; in fact, the blossoms may only open at night.

- Moths have a great sense of smell, so the flowers they are attracted to have a strong, sweet scent; again, sometimes only at night.

- The flowers typically have deep tubes to match the length of the moth's tongue.

- Because moths hover, the flowers they feed on have no landing platform.

A Sphinx Moth extracts nectar from a columbine flower.

Moth Flowers

NATIVE NECTAR PLANTS FOR ADULTS

Aquilegia species, columbines
Datura wrightii, sacred thorn-apple
Ipomoea alba, moonflower
Mirabilis species (except invasive
  M. jalapa), sweet four o'clocks
Oenothera species, evening primroses
Phlox species, phlox
Yucca species, yuccas

NONNATIVE NECTAR PLANTS FOR ADULT MOTHS

Heliotropium arborescens,
  common heliotrope
Lilium candidum, madonna lily
Matthiola bicornis, night-scented stock
Nicotiana species,
  night-blooming nicotianas
Petunia × hybrida, common
  garden petunia
Syringa vulgaris, common lilac

GIANT SILK MOTHS AND THE PLANTS THAT FEED THEIR CATERPILLARS

Cecropia—Silver maple, wild cherry, oak, sassafras, gray birch, dogwood
Luna—Hickory, maple, persimmon, sweetgum, birch, oak, alder, beech
Polyphemus—Oak, hickory, maple, birch, willow
Promethea—Wild cherry, spicebush, maple, ash, basswood, tulip tree, sweetgum, birch, sassafras

HERBS FOR ADULT MOTHS

Agastache foeniculum, anise hyssop
Borago officinalis, borage
Origanum majorana, marjoram
Origanum × *majoricum*, Italian oregano
Rosmarinus officinalis, rosemary

In search of nectar and pollen, a lesser long-nosed bat pollinates a saguaro cactus flower.

Bat Flowers

Tales about blood-sucking vampires have given bats a bad reputation. But these flying nocturnal mammals are really gentle, lovable creatures. All 45 bat species found in the U.S. and Canada feed on insects or flowers.

The vast majority of bats are insect-eating machines, so if you see them in your garden, consider yourself lucky. If not, you may be able to attract them by building or buying a bat house (see page 110 for details).

Three bat species that migrate north a thousand miles or more from their winter homes in Mexico into southern California, Arizona, New Mexico, and Texas are flower lovers, dining on nectar and pollen or fruit. They are the lesser long-nosed bat, the Mexican long-tongued bat, and the Mexican long-nosed bat. While they're feasting on the flowers, they may also pick off a few of the insects hanging out there.

These three nectarivores, as they're called, prefer a specialized diet of agave flowers and the blooms of columnar cacti native to the desert Southwest, including the saguaro. Bat flowers have to be sturdy because they take a bit of abuse: The animals typically grasp the blooms as they force their head inside, trying to reach the often copious nectar supply with their long tongue. Bats can carry huge loads of pollen on their face and fur—the better to fertilize the flowers during their evening excursions.

ANATOMY OF A BAT FLOWER

- Bats are nocturnal, so the flowers they pollinate are white- or light-colored.

- Bat flowers are night bloomers.

- Bats are mammals with a good sense of smell, and the blooms attract them with a strong, musty fragrance that resembles the scent of the bats themselves.

- The flowers must be large and strong so the bats can cling to them as they stick their noses inside the bloom.

Bat Flowers

Agave species, agaves
Carnegiea gigantea, saguaro
Pachycereus pringlei, cardon
Stenocereus thurberi, organpipe cactus

Agaves depend on bats to pollinate their flowers—which bats visit to feast on nectar.

Beetles can be a gardener's best buddies. California poppies, above, as well as the crabapple blossoms and iris on the facing page can all be pollinated by beetles.

Beetle Flowers

The British geneticist and evolutionary biologist J.B.S. Haldane quipped that "the Creator, if He exists, has an inordinate fondness for beetles." He was referring to the fact that beetles comprise 25 percent of all known animal species.

If they think about beetles at all, most gardeners see them as pests that chew holes through their prized flowers. But in addition to "bad" beetles there are gardeners' good friends, like the endearing Lady Beetle, a voracious devourer of aphids. And beetles, which come in a wide variety of body shapes and sizes, can be quite handsome and worth appreciating in their own right. They are distinguished from other insects by their two sets of wings, the outer a pair of often spectacular elytra, or protective wing cases, in bright or metallic colors with spots, stripes, and other extravagant markings.

Beetles are also important pollinators. In fact, they were probably the first practitioners of the pollination arts. Beetles achieved the pinnacle of insect evolution during the late Jurassic and early Cretaceous periods, when flowering plants were first evolving. Not surprisingly, given their reputation as garden thugs, some beetles are not the most elegant pollinators, often munching their way through petals and other flower parts and leaving their droppings in the blooms.

Anatomy of a Beetle Flower

- Beetle flowers are often large, bowl-shaped blooms.

- The blossoms are usually white or pale in color.

- Although these primeval pollinators don't have a great sense of color, beetles have a highly developed nose, and the magnolias and other ancestral flowers they still pollinate today often have a strong fruity or spicy fragrance. Carrion and dung beetles, however, prefer purple or brown flowers that smell like feces or rotting meat.

- The blooms typically don't produce a lot of nectar but have lots of pollen for beetles to dine on.

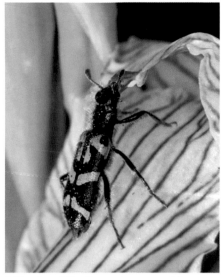

A Checkered Beetle perches on an iris flower.

Beetle Flowers

Asimina triloba, pawpaw
Calycanthus floridus, sweetshrub
Cornus species, dogwoods
Eschscholzia californica,
   California poppy

Iris species, irises
Magnolia species, magnolias
Malus species, crabapples
Nymphaea species, water-lilies
Paeonia species, peonies

Crabapple blossoms

Container Gardens for Wildlife

City dwellers, by necessity or preference, often garden solely in containers on rooftops or terraces or in window boxes. But containers have become part of the repertoire of all gardeners. Suburbanites and even rural folk, who may have acres of land, often spruce up their outdoor spaces with containers placed artistically on the patio, deck, or lawn. They too plant window boxes and suspend hanging planters from eaves and awnings.

Preplanted containers and potted plants that will appeal to hummingbirds and butterflies are available at garden centers—just use the plant lists in this volume to make sure you're buying a flower or shrub with tested wildlife appeal. But it's more fun, and usually cheaper, to make your own, combining colors and shapes that strike your fancy.

As you create a container garden for wildlife, there are a few things to keep in mind. Because you want plants that bloom for weeks and months on end, choose mostly annuals for your pots. Annuals provide virtually nonstop flowers, whereas cold-hardy perennials typically bloom for just a couple of weeks. Technically speaking, many of the "annuals" sold commercially are in fact tender perennials—including some salvias and heliotropes—that flower over long periods but won't survive the winter in cool climates.

Remember too that containers dry out fast, so you have to be attentive to the plants' needs for water. In some situations, such as hot, exposed terraces and rooftops, you may have to water daily. But don't get the wrong idea, gardening in pots is pretty easy. The size of a potted garden is contained, literally, and you'll rarely have to spend time doing one of horticulture's less pleasant chores—weeding.

Hanging baskets and other containers can be planted with annuals for continuous bloom and a steady supply of pollen and nectar for bees, butterflies, and hummingbirds.

How to Plant Containers

A container garden for wildlife has the same requirements as any garden for wildlife—flowers, sun, shelter from the wind, and water, which you will need to provide on a regular basis. Once you've chosen the spot for your pots, gather all the materials you'll require: containers, plants, potting soil, some newspaper, and mulch. Have a source of water close at hand. The best time to plant is on an overcast day or late on a sunny day, because this will give your transplants a chance to get comfortable in their new home without being stressed by the fierce midday sun. Once you have everything at hand, here's how to proceed:

- **Pick a container with drainage holes.** If the container you've chosen has no holes, you'll need to drill them. Water trapped at the bottom of a pot can cause root rot and kill your plants.

- **Line the bottom of the container with a thin layer of newspaper.** This easy barrier will allow the water to drain but prevent the soil from running out with the water.

- **Mix some potting soil with a heaping scoop of compost to help feed the plants.** Add a good foundation of soil to the container before you begin placing the flowers. How much soil to add will depend on the size of the pot in relation to the size of the plants; the goal is for the soil level to be an inch or two below the top of the pot once the plants are in.

- **Gently remove the plants from their original pots and tuck them into the soil mix.** Try not to disturb the roots too much unless the plants are root-bound. If they are, score the roots in a few places with a knife and massage the root-balls to loosen them and stimulate new growth. You can crowd the plants close together because you will be supplying all the water and nutrients they need. When all the plants are in place, fill the gaps around them with soil. Press the soil around each plant firmly.

- **Add a half-inch layer of mulch over the exposed soil.** This will help conserve water, maintain a more consistent soil temperature, and prevent soil erosion by the wind. A rough-textured mulch such as shredded bark is best because it will adhere to the soil.

- **Give your plants a healthy drink, until water starts seeping out the drainage holes.** Be sure to check the pots every day and water when it feels slightly dry.

- **Be an organic gardener.** Don't use pesticides, and apply organic fertilizers like diluted fish emulsion or compost tea every two weeks to give your plants an extra boost.

Your container garden will be all the more welcoming for wildlife if you add feeders (see page 24), nest boxes (page 105), and a birdbath or other source of water (see page 88).

For a close-up view of wildlife such as this Giant Swallowtail, plant a container with butterfly favorites such as this zinnia or the petunias in the window box on the facing page.

A WINDOW BOX

Even if your garden consists solely of a window box, you can provide an enticing buffet for butterflies, hummingbirds, and other beautiful pollinators. This design is based on a striking red and white color scheme and can be grown in full sun or partial shade. From the comfort of your own kitchen or living room you may even be able to observe caterpillars, including those of the Black Swallowtail, because the parsley included in the planting is one of its favorite foods.

Plant List

A *Pentas lanceolata*, pentas (white)
Pentas are the tallest plants in the window box design, so they're placed at the back, closest to the window. Pentas, which come in other colors as well as white, are among the best butterfly nectar plants.

B *Petroselinum crispum*, curly parsley
The attractive crinkled leaves of curly parsley knit together and form a bright green foil for the various flowers in this plan. And because it is a host plant for caterpillars, parsley also enables you to see butterflies in all their life stages.

C *Salvia elegans*, pineapple sage
Vivid red-flowered pineapple sage is probably the most widely cultivated salvia. It's also a hummingbird magnet.

D *Petunia* hybrid, petunia (white)
Petunias will captivate you with their fragrance, and these luminous white flowers are irresistible to night-flying moths.

E *Ipomoea quamoclit*, cypress vine
This lovely vine, with feathery foliage and bright red blooms, spills over the edges of the window box and provides a reason for hummingbirds to visit.

A ROUND CONTAINER

A wooden half-barrel or a plastic or terra-cotta pot of similar size is the perfect container for this planting. Nothing says "Stop here!" louder to hummingbirds than the color red, and the red flowers included in this design deliver on the promise of sweet nectar. Butterflies will also be enticed to linger. Clumps of blue fescue form a stunning backdrop for the red blooms. Use two containers to flank a doorway, or mingle them among other containers on a terrace, patio, or deck.

Plant List

A *Salvia coccinea*, scarlet sage

One specimen of impressive scarlet sage is the standout in this design. Select one of the bright red varieties that give the plant its name. If the plant gets too tall, cut it back in midsummer.

B *Zinnia elegans*, zinnia (red)

Red-flowering selections of the common zinnia, such as 'Dreamland Scarlet', are a treat for both butterflies and hummingbirds. As a bonus, goldfinches will dine on the seeds if you don't deadhead the spent blooms at the end of the season.

C *Festuca glauca*, blue fescue

This grass's porcupine-like mounds of blue-gray blades do a wonderful job of setting off all the red flowers.

D *Lotus berthelottii*, parrot's beak

A spectacular vine with an evocative name that describes the shape of its flowers, parrot's beak features not only bright red blooms but also finely textured gray foliage that cascades over the top of the container.

A RECTANGULAR PLANTER

This planter is backed by a vine-clad trellis to add height, extra interest, and privacy. The red, orange, bronze, and mahogany colors of the composites, or daisy-shape blooms, and flower clusters of the butterfly weed pick up the multicolored inflorescences of Spanish flag, which clambers up the support. This design is guaranteed to attract many butterflies and probably some hummingbirds as well. Provide multiple planters for an even more spectacular show.

Plant List

A *Ipomoea lobata*, Spanish flag

Also called firecracker vine, its tubular blooms, produced on one side of the flower stems, change color as they mature from scarlet to orange, then yellow, and finally creamy white.

B *Tithonia rotundifolia*, Mexican sunflower

An imposing specimen plant, Mexican sunflower can grow up to 6 feet tall, but shorter varieties such as 'Torch' and 'Sundance' are available. All sorts of pollinators flock to its bold orange-red flowers with yellow centers.

C *Asclepias tuberosa*, butterfly weed

A commonly available milkweed, this host plant of Monarch caterpillars features blazing orange flower clusters that attract many different adult butterflies.

D *Helianthus annuus* 'Sundance Kid', dwarf sunflower

Growing to 28 inches tall, this cultivar bears flowers 4 to 6 inches wide in combinations of pure yellow to bronze.

E *Coreopsis tinctoria* f. *atropurpurea*, red plains coreopsis

This rarer form of the plains coreopsis is 12 to 24 inches tall and covered with mahogany-red flowers.

A POTTED GARDEN

This elegant planting features flowers in dazzling shades of red and purple. A compact cultivar of songbird-favorite eastern red cedar forms a potted evergreen "hedge," adding a sense of enclosure and intimacy. Hummingbirds will be delighted by the red sage, cuphea, and purple petunias, and butterflies, bees, and other pollinators will flock to the purple heliotrope.

Plant List

A *Juniperus virginiana,* red cedar EMERALD SENTINEL ('Corcorcor')
This handsome shrub with dark green needles is perfect for a tall screen or hedge and suitable for containers. And songbirds love its fruits and dense cover. It won a Pennsylvania Horticultural Society Gold Medal Plant award.

B *Heliotropium arborescens*, heliotrope
The sweet, vanilla-scented purple flower clusters will enthrall you and a wide variety of beautiful pollinators.

C *Cuphea llavea*, red cuphea
A bushy, compact plant to 2 feet tall, it is sometimes called tiny mice or bat-face cuphea—both apt descriptions of its intriguing red and purple flowers.

D *Petunia* hybrid, petunia (purple)
These plants have three things going for them beyond their colorful, velvety flowers: their wonderful fragrance, their ability to trail over the sides of a container, and the nectar they provide for hungry pollinators.

E *Salvia greggii*, red sage
With its profusion of red tubular blooms and 3- to 4-foot height, red sage adds great presence to this planting and is one of the best ornamental plants for attracting hummingbirds and butterflies.

A Hummingbird Garden

If butterflies are the fluttering divas of the world of pollinators and bees are the workaholics, then hummingbirds are the acrobats, zipping up, down, sideways, and backward to probe long-throated, red-toned blossoms and pluck insects out of thin air. Tiny, pugnacious, and jewellike, hummingbirds are probably the most specialized nectar-eating animals. A look at hummingbirds provides a window into the elegance of adaptation in the natural world.

Hummingbirds and their favorite blooms have coevolved for mutual benefit. No matter which family they belong to, most of the flowers have a recognizable shape. This floral configuration includes a nectar bait buried inside the bloom, which means the long-billed birds must probe deeply for the sweet liquid. In the process, the hummers brush against the male and female floral parts often dangling at the flower's entrance, and pollen is deposited on their crown. When the pollen is inad-

Above: A Black-chinned Hummingbird sips nectar at a trumpet honeysuckle flower.

vertently transferred to flowers the birds subsequently visit, fertilization can occur. In return for the meal, hummingbirds play their ages-old role in the plants' survival.

Hummingbirds need nectar to support their fast-paced lifestyle. This high-energy diet provides ample fuel for flight speeds of 66 miles per hour and up to 200 wing strokes per second during the birds' courtship. And sometimes for long-distance travel—although most hummingbirds are nonmigratory or short-distance migrants, there are two exceptions. The Ruby-throated Hummingbird migrates more than 600 miles across the Gulf of Mexico to make landfall in the southeastern U.S., and many continue onward as far as Canada. The Rufous Hummingbird migrates from its winter home in Mexico as far north as Alaska. The arrival of hummingbirds in spring is timed with the blooming of nectar-producing wildflowers, including columbines.

Their incessant travels often take hummingbirds to backyard gardens. By adding hummingbird blossoms to an existing garden or creating special plantings, you can not only lure the delightful little birds but also encourage them to linger, enlivening your floral displays with their glittering colors and feisty personalities. In the process, you'll also be easing their plight, for like so many other birds and pollinators, they are vulnerable to habitat loss, pesticides, and other hazards of the modern world.

ANATOMY OF A HUMMINGBIRD FLOWER

- Hummingbird blooms tend to be red or orange, sometimes pink.
- They are typically long and tubular, adapted for a hummingbird's long, narrow bill and tongue.
- Unlike insect-pollinated flowers, they usually are not fragrant, because hummingbirds, like most birds, have a poor sense of smell.
- They provide plenty of nectar. Sugar content averages about 26 percent—about double the amount in a soft drink.
- The flowers often point downward so that hovering hummers have easy access.
- They have long stamens (the male flower parts that hold the pollen-bearing anthers) so that pollen can be deposited on the visiting bird's forehead.

The tube-shaped flower of columbine is well adapted to accommodate the bill of a hummingbird.

Ten Steps to a Hummingbird Garden

Hummingbirds are fairly easy to attract to a garden and great fun to have around. Once they discover your yard, they are likely to return at the same time every year—they have great memories. Following are ten ways to attract hummers to your garden and keep them coming.

1. **Plant lots of red, tubular flowers.** Hummingbirds are so attracted to the color that they'll check out anything red, even a toy wagon or lawn chair. Orange-red and pink also have great appeal for hummers.

2. **Observe hummingbirds in natural areas near your home to learn which flowers they love, then plant these species in your garden.** Or use the plants recommended for your region on page 78.

3. **Plant clumps of the same species, three or more, to provide as much nectar as possible.**

4. **Select plants that bloom throughout the period the birds are in your area, so they have a constant source of nectar.**

5. **Hummingbirds may seem like perpetual-motion machines, but they need places to perch and rest.** Openly branched shrubs and small trees with little branches

Red buckeye is an important nectar source for Ruby-throated Hummingbirds.

for tiny hummingbird toes are ideal, like spicebush (*Lindera benzoin*), birches (*Betula* species), and redbud (*Cercis canadensis*).

6. **Trees, shrubs, and vines with relatively large foliage offer leaves under which to huddle during rainstorms.** They also provide places where hummingbirds can sleep.

7. **If space is tight, garden vertically by growing the red-flowering vines humming-birds love, letting them clamber over fences and up trellises or lampposts.** A hummer will even visit a window box or hanging basket planted with a few of its favorite flowers—just fill them with annuals, which will bloom for months.

8. **Provide a source of water. Hummingbirds bathe often in shallow water, even in the drops that collect on leaves.** They'll also sit and preen or flit through the droplets generated by a water-conserving commercial mister.

9. **Hummers usually line their nests with soft fibers, so include some fuzzy plants in your garden.** Cinnamon fern (*Osmunda cinnamomea*) and pussy willow (*Salix discolor*) are two good examples.

10. **Lay off pesticides.** Hummingbirds can ingest these poisons when they eat insects. Systemic pesticides can also contaminate flower nectar.

Hummingbird Feeders

The best way to feed hummingbirds is to plant their favorite flowers. However, it's not harmful to use colorful red feeders filled with sugar water to lure them to places where you can easily observe them. Mix one part granulated white sugar (not honey, which promotes un-healthy fungal growth) to four parts water, then boil the solution for one or two minutes. Cool, fill the feeder, and hang it in a shady spot, where the sugar water is less likely to spoil. Clean the feeder at least once a week with a bottle brush and hot, soapy water.

Some Hummingbirds and Their Favorite Flowers

Allen's Hummingbird
Selasphorus sasin

Where they live Most migrate from Mexico to nest along the coast of California and up to southwestern Oregon.

Favorite flowers Penstemons, monkey flowers, Indian paintbrushes, California fuchsia

Anna's Hummingbird
Calypte anna

Where they live They breed from Mexico to southern Canada, east to Arizona; they winter from southern California and Arizona into Mexico.

Favorite flowers They are believed to have a close association with fuchsia-flowering gooseberry. Hummingbird sage, California Indian pink, and Indian paintbrushes are other favored blooms.

Black-chinned Hummingbird
Archilochus alexandri

Where they live They migrate from Mexico to spend the summer in central Texas and southern California north to British Columbia.

Favorite flowers Many, including trumpet creeper, scarlet hedgenettle, scarlet larkspur, and Indian paintbrushes

Calliope Hummingbird
Stelluna calliope

Where they live Calliopes, the smallest birds in North America and the world's tiniest avian migrants, winter in Mexico and spend summers from Baja to British Columbia and in the Rocky Mountains.

Favorite flowers Indian paintbrushes, penstemons, gooseberries, monkey flowers

Ruby-throated Hummingbird
Archilochus colubris

Where they live This is the only hummingbird that breeds in the midwestern and eastern U.S. and Canada. It winters from Florida and Texas south.

Favorite flowers Trumpet creeper, bee balm, trumpet honeysuckle, cardinal flower, eastern columbine, red buckeye

Rufous Hummingbird
Selasphorus rufus

Where they live These birds undertake the world's longest bird migration relative to body length—about 2,486 miles—from Mexico to as far north as Alaska.

Favorite flowers Chuparosa, ocotillo, columbine, cardinal flower, Indian paintbrushes, penstemons, gooseberries

Hummingbird Flowers for Your Region

NORTHEAST

Aquilegia canadensis, wild columbine
Ceanothus americanus, New Jersey tea
Lobelia cardinalis, cardinal flower
Lonicera sempervirens,
    coral honeysuckle
Monarda didyma, bee balm
Penstemon digitalis,
    foxglove beardtongue

SOUTHEAST

Aesculus pavia, red buckeye
Castilleja coccinea, scarlet
    Indian paintbrush
Cercis canadensis, redbud
Ipomoea quamoclit, cypress vine
Salvia lyrata, lyre-leafed sage
Silene virginica, fire pink

FLORIDA

Bignonia capreolata, cross vine
Erythrina herbea, coral bean
Hamelia patens, firebush
Hibiscus coccineus, scarlet rose mallow
Ipomopsis rubra, standing-cypress
Salvia coccinea, tropical sage

CENTRAL PRAIRIES AND PLAINS

Agastache foeniculum,
    lavender hyssop
Asclepias tuberosa, butterfly weed
Campsis radicans, trumpet creeper
Liatris species, blazingstars
Penstemon grandiflorus, beardtongue
Silene regia, royal catchfly

As they sip nectar from a favorite flower like Indian paintbrush, hummingbirds pollinate it, providing a service essential to the plant's survival.

Combine hummingbird flowers so that you have some in bloom for the entire time the little birds spend in your area. The redbud shown here provides nectar in early spring.

SOUTHWEST

Castilleja species, Indian paintbrushes
Fouquiera splendens, ocotillo
Justicia californica, chuparosa
Penstemon barbatus, scarlet bugler
Salvia greggii, red sage
Stachys coccinea, scarlet hedgenettle

CALIFORNIA

Delphinium cardinale, scarlet larkspur
Epilobium canum subsp. *latifolia*,
    California fuchsia
Keckiella cordifolia, heartleaf keckiella
Ribes speciosum,
    Fuchsia-flowering gooseberry
Salvia spathacea, hummingbird sage
Silene californica, California Indian pink

NORTHWEST

Aquilegia formosa, western columbine
Delphinium nudicaule, red larkspur
Ipomopsis aggregata, scarlet gilia
Lonicera involucrata, twinberry
Mimulus cardinalis, scarlet
    monkey flower
Ribes sanguineum, flowering currant

NONNATIVE PLANTS

Fuchsia species, fuchsias
Justicia spicigera, justicia
Kniphofia uvaria, red hot poker
Salvia elegans, pineapple sage
Tecomaria capensis, cape honeysuckle
Zinnia elegans, zinnia

A purple coneflower provides a roomy landing pad for a Tiger Swallowtail.

A Butterfly Garden

Butterflies are some of nature's most beautiful pollinators, captivating our attention with their flamboyant colors, stripes, and spots as they flutter from bloom to bloom. But while lauding bees as the intellectuals of the insect world, scientists have often dismissed butterflies as the dumb blondes. To begin with, butterflies don't buzz purposefully from flower to flower as bees do, but rather flit. This behavior, plus the fact that unlike bees they don't pollinate important crops, has led to their reputation as airheads with a pretty pair of wings. However, recent research has demonstrated that butterflies are in fact smart; they are able to learn to associate a certain flower color with a first-rate nectar supply and to improve their nectar-sipping technique with practice.

Like other flower pollinators, butterflies have coevolved with certain flowers. For example, they prefer blooms that occur in clusters, such as coneflowers and milkweeds, because these provide adequate landing pads and also allow the butterflies to walk around and sip nectar from each tiny individual flower. They do this with a long

ANATOMY OF A BUTTERFLY FLOWER

- Butterflies have good vision, so the flowers they pollinate are brightly colored, often red and orange.

- Because butterflies have a weak sense of smell, the blooms are typically odorless.

- The flowers are usually found in clusters to provide a good landing platform for the butterflies, which walk around on the flower clusters probing for nectar with their proboscises, or strawlike tongues.

- Butterfly blooms have a floral tube that is tailored to the length of the particular butterfly's tongue.

A Diana Fritillary perches on a cluster of butterfly weed flowers.

proboscis, or strawlike tongue, which uncoils to probe flowers and is coiled back up for trouble-free flying. While feeding on the nectar, adult butterflies inadvertently pollinate many plants and enable them to reproduce.

British biologist Miriam Rothschild likened a butterfly garden to a "pub"—one with nectar-laden blossoms instead of pints of ale. As you become enamored of the butterflies gracing your garden, you will want to give them incentives to linger, by providing food for their young, too. Caterpillar plants are not the same as those used by the adults. Female butterflies find the required food plants for their progeny by scratching the surface of foliage with their tarsi, or feet, and "tasting" it. Think of a caterpillar garden as a "diner," full of nutritious foliage for the rapidly growing youngsters.

If you plan a butterfly garden carefully, you can provide an oasis of habitat that can sustain the entire life cycle of some butterflies. You can also help restore the fragmented "nectar corridors," or routes followed by long-distance migrants heading south for the winter, by planting asters, goldenrods, and other late-blooming flowers. If you encourage your neighbors to plant their own butterfly gardens, you'll really be helping them not only persist in our rapidly urbanizing world but also thrive.

Butterfly weed and other nectar-rich blooms like coneflowers are irresistible to butterflies.

Ten Steps to a Butterfly Garden

With a little bit of planning and planting you can lure a variety of lovely butterflies to your yard. If you already have a sunny flower border, consider adding plants that butterflies and their caterpillars love. If you're designing a flower border from scratch, the following tips will help you create habitat for a bounty of butterflies.

1. **Locate the flower border in the sun.** Butterflies bask in the sun but avoid cool shade.

2. **Shelter the border from wind.** If necessary, create a wind block by planting a formal or informal hedge using plants that produce nectar-rich flowers.

3. **Pick plants for every season.** Butterflies need sources of flower nectar from spring through fall.

4. **Grow large clumps of three or more of each butterfly flower.**

5. **Plant a diversity of brightly colored flowers, favoring reds and oranges.** Use the plants recommended for your region on page 86.

6. **Grow caterpillar plants as well as flowers for adult butterflies.** Butterfly caterpillars, or larvae, often require a particular native plant for sustenance. (On the regional lists, plants for adults and caterpillars are listed separately.)

7. **Create a shallow puddle for swallowtails and other butterflies.** Some butterflies drink at mud puddles to obtain needed salts. Put water in a clay or plastic saucer, sprinkle on a little table salt and manure to make it more appealing, and place it in a small clearing in your flower border. See page 92.

8. **Grow weedier-looking caterpillar and nectar plants in a corner of your yard.** This will provide habitat for a wider variety of butterflies in all life stages.

9. **Provide a place for butterflies to spend the winter.** Leave seedpods and stalks of perennials as well as leaf litter. Piles of sticks, brush, logs, or old lumber will also serve as cold-weather refuges.

10. **Don't use pesticides.** Even Bt (*Bacillus thuringensis*), which is promoted as a safe and natural insecticide, kills butterfly and moth caterpillars.

The Life Cycle of a Butterfly

During their lives butterflies go through a remarkable metamorphosis. They begin life as a tiny egg. In a week or so, the caterpillar emerges and goes on an eating binge. When it has bulked up and molted several times, it stops eating, spins a silken covering, and suspends itself upside down as a pupa, or chrysalis. After a week or two the adult butterfly emerges. The four images here show the metamorphosis of a Monarch.

Some Butterflies and Their Favorite Flowers

Eastern Tiger Swallowtail
Papilio glaucus

Where they live They are found in the U.S. east of the Rockies; also southern Ontario. The Western Tiger Swallowtail, found west of the Rockies, looks similar.

Favorite flowers Bee balm, ironweed, milkweeds, sweet pepperbush for adults; black cherry, tulip tree, birches, ashes for caterpillars

Great Spangled Fritillary
Speyeria cybele

Where they live Throughout the U.S., except Florida, and southern Canada

Favorite flowers Thistles, bee balm, purple coneflower, milkweeds, joe-pye weed, ironweed, New Jersey tea for adults; violets for caterpillars

Painted Lady
Vanessa cardui

Where they live Throughout the U.S. and Canada

Favorite flowers Joe-pye weed, blazingstars, asters, goldenrods, anise hyssop for adults; many plants, but especially thistles, for caterpillars

Red Admiral
Vanessa atalanta

Where they live Throughout the U.S. and southern Canada

Favorite flowers Milkweeds, sweet pepperbush, asters, anise hyssop, coneflowers for adults; nettles for caterpillars

Common Buckeye
Junonia coenia

Where they live Buckeyes spread from the South throughout most of the U.S. as summer progresses; they are found rarely in southern Ontario and Quebec

Favorite flowers Milkweeds, asters, mints, buckwheats for adults; members of the snapdragon family, including monkey flowers, for caterpillars

Monarch
Danaus plexippus

Where they live Monarchs range throughout the U.S. and southern Canada. The long-distance champions of butterfly migration, eastern Monarchs can travel 3,000 miles from mountain fir forests west of Mexico City to their summer range in Canada.

Favorite flowers Milkweeds, asters, goldenrods, joe-pye weed, blazingstars, firebush; various milkweeds, including butterfly weed, for caterpillars

Butterfly Flowers for Your Region

NORTHEAST
Host Plants for Caterpillars
Aristolochia macrophylla,
  Dutchman's pipe
Asclepias incarnata, swamp milkweed
Ceanothus americanus, New Jersey tea
Rudbeckia species (including *R. fulgida*,
  R. hirta), yellow coneflowers
Vaccinium angustifolium,
  lowbush blueberry

Nectar Plants for Adults
Conoclinium coelestinum (syn.
  Eupatorium coelestinum), mistflower
Pycnanthemum muticum,
  mountain mint
Solidago species, goldenrods
Symphyotrichum novae-angliae, (syn.
  Aster novae-angliae) New England
  aster
Vernonia noveboracensis,
  New York ironwood

SOUTHEAST
Host Plants for Caterpillars
Baptisia australis, false indigo
Chelone glabra, white turtlehead,
Eurybia divaricata (syn. *Aster
  divaricatus*), white wood aster
Passiflora incarnata, passionflower
Solidago rugosa,
  rough-leafed goldenrod

Nectar Plants for Adults
Asclepias tuberosa, butterfly weed
Clethra alnifolia, sweet pepperbush
Echinacea purpurea, purple coneflower
Eutrochium purpureum, (syn. *Eupatorium
  purpureum*), joe-pye weed
Rudbeckia laciniata, cutleaf coneflower

FLORIDA
Host Plants for Caterpillars
Asclepias perennis, white
  swamp milkweed
Chamaecrista fasciculata, partridge pea
Lepidium virginicum, pepperweed

Phyla nodiflora, matchhead
Plumbago scandens, wild plumbago

Nectar Plants for Adults
Glandularia tampensis, Tampa vervain
Hamelia patens, firebush
Helianthus debilis, beach sunflower
Monarda punctata, dotted horsemint
Vernonia gigantea, ironweed

CENTRAL PRAIRIES AND PLAINS
Host Plants for Caterpillars
Antennaria plantaginifolia,
  plantain-leafed pussytoes
Astragalus canadensis, milk vetch
Lupinus perennis, blue wild lupine
Symphyotrichum laeve (syn. *Aster
  laevis*), smooth aster
Viola sororia, common blue violet

Nectar Plants for Adults
Agastache foeniculum, anise hyssop
Echinacea pallida, pale purple
  coneflower
Liatris species, blazingstars
Monarda fistulosa, wild bergamot
Phlox pilosa, prairie phlox

SOUTHWEST
Host Plants for Caterpillars
Acacia angustissima, fern acacia
Dalea pulchra, indigo bush
Prosopis velutina, velvet mesquite
Senna hirsuta var. *glaberrima*,
  slimpod senna
Streptanthus carinatus, twistflower

Nectar Plants for Adults
Asclepias erosa, desert milkweed
Baileya multiradiata, desert marigold
Dicliptera resupinata, twin seed
Eriogonum fasciculatum, eastern
  Mojave buckwheat
Verbena gooddingii,
  Goodding's verbena

Rudbeckia hirta, a yellow coneflower, is a host plant for caterpillars.

CALIFORNIA

Host Plants for Caterpillars:

Amorpha californica, false indigo
Arabis blepharophylla, rose rock cress
Asclepias fascicularis,
    narrowleaf milkweed
Mimulus (Diplacus) aurantiacus,
    sticky monkeyflower
Penstemon heterophyllus,
    foothill penstemon

Nectar Plants for Adults

Eriogonum latifolium,
    coastal buckwheat
Helianthus californicus,
    California sunflower
Phacelia tanacetifolia, tansy phacelia
Rudbeckia californica,
    California coneflower
Trichostema lanatum, woolly blue-curls

NORTHWEST

Host Plants for Caterpillars:

Angelica hendersonii,
    Henderson's angelica
Eriogonum umbellatum,
    sulfur buckwheat
Sedum spathulifolium, Pacific
    stonecrop
Sidalcea malviflora, checkerbloom
Sphaeralcea munroana,
    Munro's globemallow

Nectar Plants for Adults

Armeria maritima, sea thrift
Asclepias speciosa, showy milkweed
Gilia capitata, blue-headed gilia
Monardella villosa, coyote mint
Philadelphus lewisii, mock orange

Water for Wildlife

Like all living things, wildlife needs water, for drinking as well as for bathing and cooling off. And like people, many birds and other wildlife seem to simply love being around water.

Water can be an especially scarce commodity in arid areas and in cities, once the mud puddles dry up. No matter where you live, however, a reliable source of water will bring birds and other creatures to your garden, even during the times of year when water isn't in short supply. What's more, water can attract a wider variety of birds than supplemental food can; all birds need water, whereas only some birds eat seeds or suet, or are willing to perch on a feeder.

Nature provides water to wildlife in a multitude of ways that you can replicate in your home landscape. In moderate or high rainfall areas, an in-ground pool or pond may be appropriate, and countless tomes have been published in recent years with instructions on how to create them. Even a water garden in a half-barrel planter or other large container will attract good-size birds like jays, not to mention dragonflies and a variety of other fascinating insects. But although birds may drink from such sizable water features, these are too deep for bathing. For this purpose birds prefer either a natural puddle or its manmade equivalent—a birdbath. A shallow basin typically placed on a pedestal, an old-fashioned birdbath is also the simplest and one of the least expensive water sources for wildlife.

On the following pages you'll find out how to select and maintain birdbaths and other simple water features for birds ranging from large species to tiny hummers, as well as butterflies and bees.

Like other birds this Black-crested Titmouse prefers to bathe in shallow water—either a natural puddle or its manmade equivalent, a birdbath.

The Mosquito Question

There's one thing that most people ask when considering a water feature in their yard —will it attract mosquitoes? This is a legitimate question. Researchers who conducted a recent study of 10 northeastern mosquito species found that up to 80 percent of human West Nile virus infection comes from two mosquito species, both of which breed primarily in backyard sources of stagnant water, including birdbaths.

The females lay their eggs in wet areas containing even small amounts of organic matter, including leaves and animal waste. There doesn't have to be much water, either, and it only has to be around for about five days for mosquito larvae to hatch. Changing the water in your birdbath frequently will prevent the proliferation of mosquitoes. If you're creating a pond or a water garden in a container, you'll need to take other precautions, such as adding a few fish to gobble up mosquito larvae.

Birdbaths:
Questions and Answers

Not everything good under the sun is new, and this is certainly the case for birdbaths, which have been used to attract birds and adorn gardens for centuries. Used in addition to appropriate trees and shrubs and bird feeders, birdbaths are an important part of a wildlife garden, especially in arid areas and during droughts. Following are answers to some of the most commonly asked questions about them.

Q: Which birds use birdbaths?

A: Lots of them—not only birds that come to feeders but also those that appreciate a reliable source of fresh, clean water for drinking, bathing, and just cooling off during hot weather. The sound of running water will attract even more birds. You can buy a special drip hose for sound effects, or make your own by suspending a bucket with a tiny hole in the bottom above the birdbath.

Q: What kind of birdbath is best?

A: The old-fashioned kind made of molded concrete formed in two pieces, bowl and pedestal, is what most birds appear to prefer. More artsy models made of glazed ceramic, glass, metal, or plastic may look good, but that's not a bird's primary consideration. For birds, safety comes first—they don't want to fall in the water and drown, and concrete birdbaths are less slippery than the others.

Q: How deep should the water be in a birdbath?

A: To minimize the risk of drowning, the water should be less than three inches deep, and the birdbath should have a gradual, nonslippery slope. In addition, you should provide a place for the birds to perch. You can do this either by keeping the water shallow enough that the birds can safely perch in the water, or by adding a large flat stone in the center of the bowl for them to stand on.

Q: Where should I locate the birdbath?

A: Put it in a place where the birds have a 360-degree view, so they can keep an eye out for cats and other predators. Bushes and other hiding places for predators should be far enough away that the birds can escape before being pounced upon. A birdbath atop a pedestal, as opposed to one on the ground, adds an extra measure of protection.

Q: How often does the water need to be changed?

A: To prevent mosquitoes from breeding and the buildup of algae, rinse out the birdbath and add clean water every two to three days (see "The Mosquito Question," page 89). Never use additives to control algae or insects or to prevent the water from freezing. To prevent the spread of disease, immerse the birdbath in a nine-to-one water-to-bleach solution one or two times a month, and twice as often when there are disease outbreaks.

Q: Should I leave the birdbath out in winter?

A: Many backyard bird lovers haul their birdbaths indoors during the cold months, but this is precisely when water is scarcest and birds need it most. They spend a lot of time and energy searching for open water sources in winter. Portable birdbath heaters are widely available, and they use a minimal amount of electricity. You can also buy a birdbath with a built-in heater.

Birdbaths made from concrete are good for birds because they aren't slippery.

Some butterflies, such as these sulphurs, drink and get soil nutrients from puddles or damp earth.

Misters, Mud Puddles, and More

In addition to birdbaths, a few other simple devices can attract beautiful birds as well as butterflies and other beneficial insects to your garden and help sustain them. Some are available commercially, and others can even be made at home.

Misters

Because hummingbirds and others are drawn to moving water, enthusiasts often use misters to attract them. As the name suggests, they emit a fine mist of water when attached to a garden hose. If you place the mister so the water lands on the foliage of a small tree or shrub, the hummers can fly through the mist and bathe on the leaves.

Mud Puddles

Unlike hummingbirds, butterflies avoid running water, which can damage the fragile scales on their wings. Some butterflies congregate around potholes and mud puddles, or even just damp earth, where they not only drink the water but also ingest minute amounts of minerals from the soil. It's easy to make a mud puddle by clearing a sunny area of plants, leaves, or mulch, excavating a depression, and watering it often enough to keep the soil muddy. If you bury a shallow plastic trash can lid beneath the soil, it will stay wet a lot longer. Mason bees also appreciate such wet spots, where they can collect mud needed to construct their nests.

Saucer and Stones

Another way to attract butterflies is to fill a shallow plant saucer with river stones and gravel and add a small amount of water, making sure the tops of the stones remain dry so the insects can use them as perches.

Stones in a shallow container offer landing places for butterflies.

A Blooming Birdbath

Even shallow birdbaths are too deep for hummingbirds and other tiny species. These diminutive creatures often take baths in the water that collects on plant leaves. One of the most spectacular natural birdbaths is the cup plant, *Silphium perfoliatum*. This native of the central and eastern U.S. and southeastern Canada has large leaves that clasp its square stems to form little cups, hence its name. The cups catch and store rainwater, often for several days. From mid- to late summer the plant's beautiful yellow blooms are an added bonus. Cup plant occurs naturally in moist environments but does fine when planted in fertile medium soils, in full sun to partial shade. It's an impressive plant that can grow up to eight feet tall when it has plenty of room. Other plants with large leaves, including maples, also serve as natural birdbaths.

Hummingbirds sip water that collects in the leaf axils of cup plants.

A Buffet for Beneficial Insects

One of the reasons so many gardens have pest problems is that they're not very inviting to predators and parasites, which in healthy ecosystems keep harmful insects in check. The most effective way to welcome these beneficial insects is to grow their favorite flowers. The blooms they love best include the inverted parasol-shaped inflorescences called umbels produced by popular culinary herbs like dill and parsley, as well as the daisylike native wildflowers technically known as composites.

Beneficial insects not only devour and destroy many of the pests that ravage prized garden plants, they also offer a diverse new world of fascinating creatures for you to discover. Some of these species are old friends, such as bright red lady beetles. Some are quite beautiful, such as delicate green lacewings. Other predators look the part, including the spined soldier bug, which is shaped like a shield, with a conspicuous spine on each shoulder, armorlike plates for wings, and a sharp beak it uses to impale its victims.

To maximize insect diversity and predator power in your garden, mingle their favored blooms in your planting beds, or mass them to create predator patches in the more infested areas in your yard. Even a few plantings of umbel flowers or composites can provide nectar for dozens of tiny flies and wasps, each capable of destroying hundreds of pestiferous insects. Just remember that if you want to see lovely lacewings and brutal-looking soldier bugs at work, you have to lay off the pesticides.

Plant asters and goldenrods in your garden to help deter insect pests.

A harvestman patrols a sweetshrub flower seeking pests to eat. Together with beneficial insects harvestmen and spiders keep insect pests in check.

Ten Steps to a Predator-Friendly Garden

A number of so-called biological pest controls, the fancy term for beneficial insects, are sold at local nurseries and mail-order suppliers. But a better and less expensive approach is to let nature truly take its course—invite a wide variety of these horticultural "good guys" that already live in your area into your garden to gobble up the "bad guys." Here's how to make your property predator friendly.

1. **Identify before you squish or swat.** Some beneficial insects, like lady beetles, are instantly recognizable, but others are unfamiliar or scary looking, and a few are almost microscopic. Buy a good guide to beneficial insects and use it to distinguish the good guys from the pests.

2. **Grow their favorite flowers.** Some blooms are particularly attractive to many beneficial insects, particularly composites and umbels. See page 100 for plant recommendations.

3. **Stagger the plantings so that some predator-friendly flower or other is always in bloom to provide nutritious pollen and sweet nectar.**

4. **Grow predator-friendly plants of various heights.** Create the kind of structurally

diverse habitat that will attract an array of good guys in your garden to chomp on or parasitize a wide variety of pests.

5. **Leave the leaves in your planting beds.** A healthy layer of leaf litter provides habitat for beetles, spiders, and other important predators.

6. **Provide a source of water.** This can range from a pond to a birdbath to a shallow dish filled with pebbles and water.

7. **Give your beneficials some shelter from the wind and rain with a hedge, tall perennials, or sunflowers.**

8. **Don't use pesticides.** These cause as much harm to the beneficial insects as to the pests.

9. **Invite birds and bats into your garden.** These insect eaters appreciate trees, shrubs with berries, nectar-producing flowers, water features, and nest boxes.

10. **Tolerate minor pest infestations.** Normal populations of bad guys are a necessary food source for the beneficials and help keep them in your garden.

ANATOMY OF A PREDATOR-FRIENDLY FLOWER

- Most beneficial insects eat pollen and nectar in at least one of their life stages and are drawn to plants with clusters of closely spaced flowers that provide these important foods.

- The inflorescences provide them with an attractive landing pad. In a typical umbel, individual flower stalks are topped by hundreds of diminutive florets that together form a platform.

- Beneficials, notably the thousands of different mini-wasps, tend to be petite. The nectar of most flowers is recessed beyond the reach of their minuscule tongues, so they seek out flowers that are small and shallow enough for them.

- Umbelliferous plants typically have white or yellow flowers.

Umbels like this dill flower are popular with predators such as tiny wasps.

Some Good Guys

Predators

Most predators are insects that catch and eat other insects, mites, and other garden pests. Among the predators that are gardeners' best friends are beetles, true bugs, lacewings, syrphid flies, as well as spiders and harvestmen. Typically, adult insects dine on pollen and nectar from umbels and other favored flowers (see page 100), while the larvae do the heavy-duty pest control.

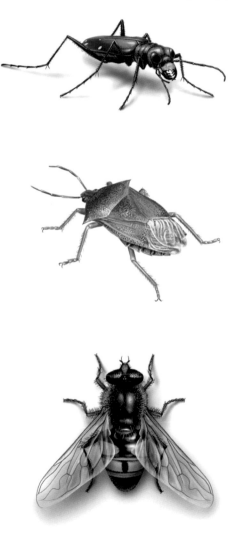

Beetles

Ladybugs, technically beetles, are probably the best-known beneficial insects. Their alligatorlike larvae are voracious aphid eaters. But many other beetles also feed on garden pests. Other notable examples are rove beetles, ground beetles, and tiger beetles.

True Bugs

Many insects are commonly called bugs, but true bugs are a group with mouthparts adapted for piercing and sucking the eggs and larvae of other species. Bigeyed bugs, minute pirate bugs, and the Spined Soldier Bug are notable examples.

Lacewings

The larvae of green lacewings and the less commonly observed brown lacewings are fierce predators of nuisance species, especially aphids; in fact, they're known as aphid lions. The adults have beautiful diaphanous wings.

Syrphid Flies

Immature syrphid flies (also called flower or hover flies) can consume as many as 50 or 60 aphids an hour. They look like little bees but are slightly darker and do a lot of hovering and darting.

Harvestmen

Also known as daddy longlegs, these arachnids have a short, globular body and eight long, slender legs. Harvestmen eat aphids, beetle larvae, small slugs, and other soft-bodied pests.

Top to bottom: An adult tiger beetle, a Spined Soldier Bug, and a syrphid fly, sizes not to scale.

Parasitoids

Parasitoids are insects with an immature life stage, usually egg or larva, that develops on or within a host, ultimately killing it—hence their value as pest control. Whereas insect predators immediately kill or disable their prey, pests attacked by parasitoids die more slowly. The following four types of mini-wasps, which are harmless to humans, and tachinid flies are among the parasitoids you should invite to your garden.

Aphidiid Wasps

These tiny black wasps attack only aphids. You'll know they're around when you see tan aphid "mummies"—swollen, dead aphids that have been hardened to form a protective case for the wasps' developing pupae.

This moth caterpillar has been parasitized by braconid wasps. The white knobs are wasp pupae.

Braconid Wasps

If you see a dying aphid or caterpillar with small white or yellow cocoons on its back, you are most likely witnessing the work of these small wasps.

Chalcid Wasps

This large group of tiny wasps parasitizes the eggs and larvae of scale insects, whiteflies, and other pests. The adults feed on some of these garden pests and lay their eggs on or in others.

Trichogramma Wasps

Trichogrammas are microscopic wasps that lay their eggs in the eggs of other insects, including those of armyworms, cankerworms, loopers, leaf rollers, webworms, and gypsy moths.

Tachinid Flies

A large and very variable family of medium to large true flies, tachinids lay their eggs on the caterpillars of various pests.

A trichogramma wasp (middle) and a tachinid fly (bottom), sizes not to scale.

The Best Blossoms for Beneficial Insects

Native Wildflowers

Studies suggest that native composites, members of the aster family, are champions at attracting beneficial insects. Composites are plants with daisylike blooms consisting of tiny flowers packed together on a central disk and surrounded by colorful ray flowers. North America is home to a large variety of spectacular composites. Some of the most widely distributed are described below. Buckwheats (*Eriogonum* species) and milkweeds (*Asclepias* species), members of the smartweed and milkweed families, respectively, also attract good bugs.

Asters

One aster or another is found in all 50 states. Asters come in blues, purples, and pinks, all with a yellow center. Expect to see some labeled as *Aster*, some as *Symphyotrichum,* and others as *Eurybia*, as the genus *Aster* is split up into several smaller genera.

Coneflowers

In colors ranging from purple to gold, typically with brown to orange centers, coneflowers, the common name for *Echinacea*, *Rudbeckia*, and *Ratibida* species, are found from coast to coast.

Goldenrods

Some of the most ubiquitous composites and easily recognized by their golden inflorescences with dense masses of tiny flowers, goldenrods (*Solidago* species) are often difficult to tell apart.

Tickseeds

Tickseeds, or *Coreopsis* species, are native to all but three states—Alaska, Nevada, and Utah. They are often at least partly yellow and have petals with notched tips.

Sunflowers

Helianthus species, wild relatives of cultivated sunflowers, which are known for their huge flower heads, are found throughout the U.S. Often yellow, they also occur in shades of orange, chestnut, and maroon, sometimes in combination.

Popular with beneficial insects, composites like these asters have a central disk of nectar-rich flowers surrounded by colorful sterile ray flowers.

Culinary Herbs

Members of the carrot or parsley family, with distinctive flower clusters called umbels that resemble little upside-down umbrellas, have long been important crop plants. In recent times they've also been recognized for their ability to attract all sorts of beneficial insects, predatory bugs in particular. Following are a few culinary umbels of varying heights and forms to create a diversity of habitats for good bugs.

Cilantro is equally popular with cooks and beneficial insects.

Cilantro, coriander

Coriander is the name of the seeds, and the leaves are known as cilantro. Umbels of small white to pale pink flowers appear in midsummer. In one study coriander (botanically known as *Coriandrum sativum*) beat ten other plants in attracting aphid-eating syrphid flies. Height: 1 to 3 feet.

Chervil

A short, mound-forming herb, chervil (*Anthriscus cerefolium*) prefers a cool, shady spot. Its delicate ferny leaves have a mild, aniselike flavor. One writer likened its pinkish-white umbels to "exquisite bits of enamel work." Height: 1 to 2 feet.

Parsley

Cooks value the flavorful emerald-green leaves of flat-leaf parsley (*Petroselinum crispum* var. *neapolitanum*), and beneficial insects love its beautiful yellow blossoms. Parsley also supports the caterpillars of Black and Anise Swallowtails. Height: 2 feet.

Dill

Prized for its feathery foliage and tasty seeds, dill (*Anethum graveolens*) also produces golden umbels. Among the predators it lures are lacewings. Black and Anise Swallowtails feast on the foliage. Height: 1½ to 3 feet.

Lovage

Lovage (*Levisticum officinale*) looks like a gargantuan celery plant. In summer it produces umbels of tiny yellow flowers. This giant is big enough to support you as well as tiny wasps and swallowtail butterflies-to-be. Height: 3 to 5 feet.

Housing Projects

By destroying so much of their habitat, we've deprived wildlife not only of food but also places to live. Fortunately, homemade or store-bought houses are acceptable substitutes for many species, as you'll discover on the following pages. Just don't waste your time or money on butterfly hibernation boxes, which won't work.

In the heavily developed areas of their range, Purple Martins readily nest in artificial birdhouses—provided they are designed just right for this communally nesting bird.

Birdhouses: Questions and Answers

Birdhouses have become some of the most popular garden ornaments. A big selection of sizes and styles is available, from rustic twig "cabins" to ornate Victorian "cottages." Fanciness is more important to you than to your feathered friends. All they care about is their safety, and a box just big enough to house their brood. Here are the answers to some commonly asked questions about how to buy or build a suitable birdhouse, technically known as a nest box.

Q: Do all birds use nest boxes?

A: No. Birdhouses are used mostly by so-called secondary cavity nesters—species that select an available cavity but don't excavate their own. However, these birds come in all shapes and sizes, from chickadees to turkey vultures.

Q: What is the best way to select a birdhouse?

A: The first things to do are to find out which species in your area will nest in birdhouses, decide which one you want to house, and make sure its preferred habitat is in your garden or nearby.

Q: How big should a birdhouse be?

A: There is no one-size-fits-all birdhouse. A nest box needs to be suited to the particular species you want to attract. The dimensions to consider are size of the box floor, box height, height of the entrance, and diameter of the entrance. The latter is extremely important—too small and the bird won't fit in, but too large and predators will be able to move in or snatch eggs or nestlings. How high to place the birdhouse is another important consideration. See pages 105–109 for specifics.

Q: What special features should I look for?

A: Wood is the best building material—it's durable, it's well insulated, and it breathes. Birdhouses should have some small holes, typically in the floor, for drainage, and more small holes, typically in the sides of the box just below the roof, for ventilation. They should also be easily opened, preferably from the top, so you can clean them out. Some birds will build a new nest on top of an old one, but it's best to clean out your birdhouses every year after the nesting season.

Populations of Mountain Chickadees have declined significantly over the past 30 years. Gardeners can help by putting up birdhouses in areas where the bird occurs.

Q: Should birdhouses have perches below the entrance hole?

A: Never. Perches provide starlings and other predators with a convenient place to wait for lunch.

Q: How can I protect my birds from predators?

A: Proper size, especially the entrance hole, is the first line of defense. Birdhouses mounted on metal poles are the most difficult for cats, squirrels, raccoons, and other predators to reach. Nest boxes on trees are safer if you wrap a sheet-metal guard around the trunk. Lining the entrance hole with sheet metal prevents squirrels from gnawing their way inside the house.

Q: Which way should a birdhouse face?

A: It should never face a busy street or highway, or even an area frequented by people where the birds will be disturbed often. Generally, in hot climates the hole should face north or east to avoid overheating, while in cold climates a south-facing hole may help keep the inhabitants cozy.

Nest Box Dimensions

The size of both a nest box itself and the entrance is crucial in determining which birds use it. If you wish to attract a specific bird species to your nest box, follow the recommended sizes listed here—and be sure the bird nests in your area.

SPECIES	FLOOR (IN.)	WOOD CHIPS ON FLOOR	HEIGHT (IN.)	ENTRANCE ABOVE FLOOR (IN.)	DIAMETER OF ENTRANCE (IN.)	FEET ABOVE GROUND OR WATER (W)	PREFERRED HABITAT CODES §
Wood Duck	12×12	yes	22	17	4	20–10, 6W	3, 5
Hooded Merganser	10×10	yes	15–18	10–13	5	4–6	3, 5
American Kestrel	8×8	yes	12–15	9–12	3	10–30	1, 4
Barn Owl	10×18	yes	15–18	0–4	6	12–18	4
Barred Owl	12×12	yes	20–24	14	6×6	15–20	5
Screech Owl (Eastern, Western)	8×8	yes	12–15	9–12	3	10–30	2
Golden-fronted Woodpecker	6×6	yes	12	9	2	10–20	2
Downy Woodpecker	4×4	yes	9	7	1¼	5–15	2
Northern Flicker	7×7	yes	16–18	14–16	2½	6–30	1, 2
Great Crested Flycatcher	6×6	yes	8–10	6–8	1$\frac{9}{16}$*	8–20	1, 2
Ash-throated Flycatcher	6×6	yes	8–10	6–8	1½*	8–20	1, 6
Tree Swallow	5×5	no	6–8	4–6	1½*	4–15	1
Violet-green Swallow	5×5	no	6–8	4–6	1½*	4–15	1
Chickadees	4×4	yes	9	7	1⅛	4–15	2
Titmice	4×4	yes	9	7	1¼	5–15	2
Nuthatches	4×4	yes	9	7	1⅜	5–15	2
Carolina Wren	4×4	no	6–8	4–6	1½*	5–10	2, 7
Bewick's Wren	4×4	no	6–8	4–6	1¼	5–10	2, 7
House Wren	4×4	no	6–8	4–6	1–1¼	4–10	2, 7
Bluebird (Eastern, Western)	4×4	no	8–12	6–10	1½*	3–6	1
Mountain Bluebird	4×4	no	8–12	6–10	1$\frac{9}{16}$*	3–6	1

* Precise measurement required; if diameter is larger, starlings may usurp cavity.

§ Preferred habitat codes: **1.** Open areas in the sun (not shaded permanently by trees), pastures, fields, or golf courses. **2.** Woodland clearings or the edge of woods. **3.** Above water, or if on land, the entrance should face water. **4.** On trunks of large trees or high in little-frequented parts of barns, silos, water towers, or church steeples. **5.** Moist forest bottomlands, flooded river valleys, swamps. **6.** Semiarid country, deserts, dry open woods, and wood edge. **7.** Backyards, near buildings. **8.** Near water; under bridges, barns. **9.** Mixed conifer-hardwood forests.

Chart adapted from Daniel D. Boone, *Homes for Birds*. Conservation Bulletin 14, 1979; also Susan E. Quinlan, *Bird Houses for Alaska*, vol. 1, no. 3, Alaska Wildlife Watcher's Report, Alaska Department of Fish and Game, 1982.

Like all good nest boxes, this home of a Prothonotary Warbler comes without a perch below the entrance hole—so there is no convenient place for a predator to wait for lunch.

Most Wanted Birds

In 2001, the Birdhouse Network (TBN), coordinated by the Cornell Lab of Ornithology, identified 16 "most wanted" bird species and asked citizen scientists to place nest boxes in their yard or neighborhood and monitor the birds that nest inside. Data suggest that six of the birds have experienced statistically significant population declines. You can help by putting out birdhouses for these species. Following is information on the six birds, where they live, and the required nest box dimensions. You can become a citizen scientist by monitoring any nesting attempts and adding your observations to the Cornell Lab's database, which you can access via nestwatch.org.

Prothonotary Warbler

Commonly called the Golden Swamp Warbler, the Prothonotary has a brilliant orange-yellow head and neck and olive upper back. Its breast and belly are yellow fading to buff, and the edges of its wings are bluish gray. Data show a population decline of 2.7 percent a year throughout their breeding range from 1980 to 1999.

Range Breeds throughout the eastern U.S. and in southern Canada.

Habitat Areas with stagnant water, such as swamps, ponds, and lowland forests subject to flooding.

Nest Box Dimensions Box floor: 5 by 5 inches; height: 6 inches; entrance height: 4 to 5 inches; entrance diameter: 1 1/8 inches; placement height: 4 to 6 feet

Be sure to put the house in a shady area near water or, even better, *over* water to stymie predators.

Mountain Chickadee

You can tell this chickadee from the more common Black-capped Chickadee by the white stripe above its eyes. Data suggest the Mountain Chickadee has declined 25 to 30 percent over the past 30 years.

Range Lives year-round in the western U.S. and Canada. Breeds above 5,000 feet.

Habitat Montane coniferous forests, especially spruce-fir, pine, and pinyon-juniper. Mountain chickadees visit feeders for seed and suet.

Nest Box Dimensions Box floor: 4 by 4 inches; height: 8 to 10 inches; entrance height: 6 to 8 inches; entrance diameter: 1 1/8 inches; placement height: 4 to 15 feet

Nestlings suffer high rates of predation, so erect predator guards (see page 104) and put a metal plate around the entrance hole to prevent rodents from enlarging it. Cover the bottom of the box with 1 inch of wood shavings.

Oak Titmouse

This small titmouse is uniformly gray or brownish gray, without the black face and head markings of the Tufted or Bridled Titmouse. Until recently, it and the Juniper Titmouse were

The loss of natural cavities suitable for nesting is affecting the populations of Oak Titmouse.

considered one species, the Plain Titmouse. According to TBN, the Oak Titmouse declined 1.8 percent a year from 1980 to 1999.

Range California north to southern Oregon and south to northern Baja.

Habitat Open, dry woods, often but not exclusively oak woodlands. Visits shade trees in gardens.

Nest Box Dimensions Box floor: 4 by 4 inches; height: 10 to 12 inches; entrance height: 6 to 10 inches, entrance diameter: 1 1/8 inches; placement height: 5 to 15 feet

Brown-headed Nuthatch
The Brown-headed Nuthatch is smaller than both the White-breasted and Red-breasted Nuthatch and has a brown cap. Like all nuthatches, it is acrobatic, hopping along tree trunks and branches, often upside down. But it is the only North American bird observed to regularly use a tool while foraging: Grasping a piece of bark in its bill, it pries up other bark to expose tasty insects hidden underneath. Data show the bird population has declined 45 percent over the past 35 years.

Range Southeast and Gulf Coast states from Delaware to Texas.

Habitat Pine and mixed pine-hardwood forests, often in clearings or along forest edges. Although its habitat requirements are quite specific, the Brown-headed Nuthatch will nest in snags and nest boxes in residential areas as long as mature pines are available within a few hundred feet.

Nest Box Dimensions Box floor: 4 by 4 inches; height: 8 to 10 inches; entrance height: 6 to 8 inches; entrance diameter: 1 1/4 inches; placement height: 4 to 6 feet

Even though Brown-headed Nuthatches are very specific in their habitat needs, they will use nest boxes in residential areas provided they are near mature pines, on which the birds depend.

According to TBN, it is a good idea to attach predator guards. The bird nests relatively low, making it vulnerable to predators. If possible, provide several nest boxes because the bird is known to start nests in multiple cavities before eventually settling in one.

Purple Martin

The largest North American swallow, the glossy, bluish-black Purple Martin, which nests communally, has long entertained people with its social antics. The birds have taken to artificial structures so readily that in the East they almost always nest in birdhouses and gourds. Yet data show that in some areas, such as the central U.S., populations have still declined by more than 50 percent.

Range Breeds along the West Coast, in Arizona, New Mexico, Utah, and Colorado, and throughout the eastern and central U.S. and Canada.

Common in rural as well as urban areas and found in many different habitats, Eastern Screech Owls readily make their nests in birdhouses.

Habitat Open and semiopen areas, including parks, pastures, towns, and suburbs. In the interior West, Purple Martins are less likely to inhabit nest boxes, relying more heavily on natural tree cavities.

Nest Box Dimensions Purple Martins nest in multilevel structures with multiple entrances. For this reason, and because they nest in groups and return to the same site each year, establishing a new colony is more complex than housing other songbirds. For detailed instructions and readymade houses and gourd racks, see the website of the Purple Martin Conservation Association, www.purplemartin.org.

Eastern Screech Owl

This small, eight-inch owl comes in two color "morphs": The northern birds are mainly gray and southerners are rufous. The breast and belly of both are heavily streaked and spotted with black. All eastern screech owls have yellow eyes and prominent ear tufts. According to TBN, populations declined 1.3 percent per year from 1980 to 1999.

Range East of the Rocky Mountains to the Atlantic.

Habitat Forests of all types, especially those with clearings and fields nearby for hunting. They also inhabit parks and gardens. Although their descending whinny and trill are often heard, they are rarely seen because they hunt at night.

Nest Box Dimensions Box floor: 8 by 8 inches; height: 12 to 15 inches; entrance height: 9 to 12 inches; entrance diameter: 3 inches; placement height: 10 to 30 feet

Bat Houses

There are several good reasons for installing a bat house on your property. Bats are fascinating creatures, and a single animal can eat thousands of mosquitoes a night. As a bonus, if you put a shallow tray or plant saucer underneath a bat house you can collect guano—free fertilizer—for your flower beds. Bats are very particular about their roosting spaces, so it pays to read up on their requirements before buying or building a bat house. Detailed information available on the Bat Conservation International website (www.batcon.org) is backed up by years of research. Following are a few important tips:

- Bat houses should be big—2 feet tall at a minimum, with as many roosting chambers as possible, each at least 14 inches wide and spaced 3/4 to 1 inch apart. A four-chamber wooden model for sale in Batcon's online store, which can house more than 300 bats, is 32 inches tall, 20 inches wide, and 6 inches deep, with a back wall that extends below the open bottom to provide a landing platform. It has a shingled roof to keep the mammals dry, and grooved surfaces for gripping. Mount the bat house at least 12 feet above the ground, on buildings or poles.

- Bats want to be warm. Other than house size, temperature is the most important criterion. Full-day sun is recommended in all but the hottest climates; and throughout the U.S., except the desert Southwest and central Texas, the houses should be painted a dark or medium color for extra heat absorption.

- Location, location, location: Most nursery colonies of bats roost within a quarter mile of water.

Bats are picky when it comes to the right place to roost. Be sure to follow the guidelines for size and placement when you install a bat house. And be prepared to wait for them to move in.

Bee Houses

Although providing pollen and nectar for busy bees is important, a lack of nesting sites is probably a bigger threat than a dearth of flowers, according to the Xerces Society's Pollinator Conservation Program. Here's how we gardeners can help:

- **Leave patches of bare ground where they can burrow.** About two-thirds of North America's bee species nest in the ground.

- **Leave logs, snags, or dead branches in your yard.** Most of the bees that do not nest in the ground nest in beetle holes in dead trees or limbs.

- **Buy or build a nesting block for solitary nesting bees.** Always use preservative-free lumber (see www.xerces.org/Pollinator_Insect_Conservation/nativebeenests.pdf for details). In a solid block of wood at least 4 inches deep and 8 inches long, drill different-size nesting holes for various bee species. Make the holes 3/32 to 3/8 inch in diameter and as deep as possible while keeping one end closed, and smooth inside. Space the holes 3/4 inch apart from center to center. Attach the block to a fence or building facing east or southeast; bees need the warmth of the morning sun to get going each day.

- **Construct or buy some boxes for bumblebee colonies.** They should be about 7 by 7 by 7 inches, with a few ventilation holes drilled on the sides near the top and drainage holes in the bottom, all covered with screening to keep ants out. Make an entrance tunnel by drilling a hole in one side and inserting 3/4-inch plastic pipe. Fill the box with a soft, fluffy material like cotton, and put it in a dry spot on the ground in a flower bed.

Solitary nesting bees are the tenants of this simple homemade nesting block.

For More Information

Online Resources

Brooklyn Botanic Garden
For articles on wildlife gardening visit
bbg.org/wildlife

Lady Bird Johnson Wildflower Center
Database of native wildflowers searchable
by region and growing conditions
www.wildflower.org

National Wildlife Federation
Backyard habitat certification program
www.nwf.org/backyard

Bats

Bat Conservation International
www.batcon.org

Birds

Cornell Lab of Ornithology
www.birds.cornell.edu

U.S. Fish and Wildlife Service Bird
Pamphlets
www.fws.gov/migratorybirds/pamphlet/
pampletes.html

Bees, Butterflies, Moths, and More

BugGuide.net
Identification, images, and information
www.bugguide.net

Journey North
An educational website that engages children
in the study of wildlife migration worldwide
www.learner.org/jnorth

The Lepidopterists' Society
Links to sites for butterflies and moths
www.lepsoc.org

Monarch Watch
Education, conservation, and research
www.monarchwatch.org

North American Butterfly Association
www.naba.org

What's That Bug
Identification help, images, and information
www.whatsthatbug.com

The Xerces Society
Invertebrate conservation
www.xerces.org

Books

Field Guides

Kaufman Field Guide to Insects of North America
By Kenn Kaufman and Eric Eaton
Houghton Mifflin, 2007

National Audubon Society Field Guide Series
Guides to North American birds; butterflies; insects and spiders; trees; wildflowers; and more

Petersen Guide Series
Guides to North American birds; butterflies and moths; caterpillars; insects; trees; wildflowers; and more
Houghton Mifflin

Stokes Beginner's Guide Series
Guides to North American bats, butterflies, dragonflies, hummingbirds, and more
Little, Brown & Company

BBG Handbooks on Related Topics

Bird Gardens, 1998
The Butterfly Gardener's Guide, 2003
Butterfly Gardens, 2007 (revised edition)
Gardening With Children, 2007
Hummingbird Gardens, 2007 (revised edition)

To read excerpts of these and other titles, visit bbg.org/handbooks.
To order books go to shop.bbg.org or call 718-623-7286.

Contributors

Janet Marinelli is the former director of publishing at Brooklyn Botanic Garden. She has written extensively about biological invasion and other conservation issues. She serves on the steering committee of the Center for Urban Restoration Ecology and the plant conservation committee of the American Public Garden Association. Her latest book, *Plant* (Dorling Kindersley, 2005), showcases 2,000 species worldwide that are threatened in the wild but alive and well in gardens and makes the case that gardens can play an important role in saving plants. Since its debut in the U.S., the book has been published in more than a dozen countries around the world. Marinelli has won numerous awards for her writing, including the American Horticultural Society's prestigious American Gardener Award for writing "that has made a significant contribution to horticulture."

Photos

Dave Allen page 25 (3)

Rick & Nora Bowers BowersPhoto.com pages 63 (top), 81, 83 (4)
R. & N. Bowers/Vireo page 37, 72

David Cavagnaro pages 2, 4, 7, 12, 13 (top three), 18, 19 (left), 20, 32, 33 (top), 36, 37, 45, 46, 47, 55, 58 (and back cover), 59, 67, 80, 92, 93 (top), 95, 96 (and back cover), 97, 101

J. Culbertson/Vireo page 29

R. & S. Day/Vireo pages 22, 24 (and back cover), 33 (bottom)

Alan & Linda Detrick cover, pages 13 (bottom), 14, 56, 57, 63 (bottom), 73, 78, 79, 87, 91, 100

Derek Fell page 11

S. Greer/Vireo page 38

D. Huntington/Vireo page 105

G. McElroy/Vireo page 10

A. Morris/Vireo page 102

R. Nussbaumer/Vireo page 89

Jerry Pavia pages 15, 16, 19 (right), 21, 42 (2), 43, 52, 53, 54, 62, 65, 66, 74, 75, 82, 93 (bottom)

S. & S. Rucker/Vireo page 106

Jane Ruffin page 99

J. Schumacher/Vireo page 28

R. & A. Simpson/Vireo page 109

Brian E. Small/Vireo page 107

H.P. Smith, Jr./Vireo page 8

Merlin D. Tuttle/Bat Conservation International pages 60, 61, 110

Mace Vaughan/The Xerces Society page 111

A. Walther/Vireo page 41

J. Wedge/Vireo page 108

Illustrations

Steve Buchanan

Index

PROVIDING EXPERT GARDENING ADVICE FOR OVER 60 YEARS

Join Brooklyn Botanic Garden as an annual Subscriber Member and receive our next three gardening handbooks delivered directly to you, plus *Plants & Gardens News*, *BBG Members News*, and reciprocal privileges at many botanic gardens across the country. Visit bbg.org/subscribe for details.

BROOKLYN BOTANIC GARDEN ALL-REGION GUIDES

World renowned for pioneering gardening information, Brooklyn Botanic Garden's award-winning guides provide practical advice in a compact format for gardeners in every region of North America. To order other fine titles, call 718-623-7286 or shop online at shop.bbg.org. For additional information about Brooklyn Botanic Garden, call 718-623-7200 or visit bbg.org.